1996
GREEN
COIN
BOOK

Twenty-Third Edition

A complete, illustrated catalog of U.S. coins
and bills and their cash premium values
from 1652 to the present
and
The complete coinage of Canada and Newfoundland
from 1858 to date

BY ROBERT FRIEDBERG
EDITED BY ARTHUR L. AND IRA S. FRIEDBERG

Associate Editor: Arthur S. Goldenberg

WINGS BOOKS
New York • Avenel, New Jersey

This 1995 edition is published by Wings Books,
distributed by Random House Value Publishing, Inc.,
40 Engelhard Avenue, Avenel, New Jersey 07001, by
arrangement with Mr. Arthur L. Friedberg and Mr. Ira S. Friedberg.

Originally published as *The Green Coin Book Appraising and
Selling Your Coins*

Printed and bound in the United States of America

ISBN 0-517-12301-0
8 7 6 5 4 3 2 1

CONTENTS

Contents

A Note from the Publisher

The cash premium values in this book are published for the information and guidance of all concerned—for those who have coins for sale as well as for those who want a complete reference work on the market value of coins and currency.

The valuations listed do not indicate retail prices, but instead, closely approximate how much established coin dealers will actually pay for any material needed in their stock. The valuations are based on the coins being in Good to Very Good condition, unless otherwise noted. Coins in better condition are worth more.

The editors are professional coin dealers. Anyone interested in either buying or selling coins and paper money may contact them at the following address: The Coin & Currency Institute, Inc., P.O. Box 1057, Clifton, NJ 07014. When shipping coins, be sure to use insured or registered mail.

Since silver and gold have risen to their current levels, the values of many coins are based on their precious metal content. Most coin dealers are paying a premium over face value for any and all of these silver coins regardless of date or condition; in many cases, even uncirculated coins are not worth more than their melt value. For the purpose of this book, silver has been calculated at $4.75 per ounce, and gold at $375.00 per ounce. Therefore, all dimes, quarters and half dollars which are valued at $.28, $.68, $.70 and $1.40 respectively, and many United States gold coins, fluctuate in relation to the commodity price of silver and gold and their actual premium value will vary accordingly.

Because of this, the cash premium values of silver coins, dollars, Commemorative Half Dollars, Proof & Mint sets and gold coins are subject to fluctuation.

Do not clean or polish any coins! They will lose a great deal of their premium value if you do. Coins should be left in the same condition as when found, no matter how dark they may appear.

Preface

At some time or another almost all of us acquire or come across some coins or old pieces of paper money which excite our curiosity or otherwise hold our interest. What is it about these coins that has thus captured our attention? It may have been the strangeness of denomination (a copper 2 Cent piece or a nickel 3 Cent piece or a silver Half Dime or a 3 Dollar gold piece); it may have been antiquity (a large Cent of 1794 or a Colonial Copper of 1694); or the surprise of discovering for yourself an untoward bit of information (that we once used a 15 Cent piece of paper money that was, and still is, legal tender); it may have been sheer, compelling intrinsic value (any gold coin) or immediate negotiable value (an old large size 5 Dollar bill); or it may have been the historical associations evoked by the coins (the Battle of Gettysburg, the exploits of Daniel Boone, the Landing of the Pilgrims, the discovery of America itself); or perhaps it was the glittering beauty of perfection (a set of current coins in brilliant proof condition, or a single older coin so finely preserved that it assumed the status of a gem in your mind).

No matter which quality it has been, or what circumstance introduced you to the coins, you have held them in your hand, you have scrutinized them (perhaps under a magnifying glass), you have conjured with them in your imagination, and after the first flush of recognition has passed and the pride of ownership has asserted itself, one question, one unknown factor still remains unanswered for you—how much are these coins worth? It is at this point that for you

THE SEARCH FOR RARE COINS

has begun, a pursuit, or pastime, if you will, indulged in passionately by millions of us for pleasure or for profit. That your coins are worth more than their face value, there is somehow no doubt in your mind. You have been conditioned to believe it, or at the least, to hope it, by the larger and larger amounts of rare coin publicity in recent years.

A boy, rummaging around among his grandmother's effects, finds an 1856 Flying Eagle Cent and sells it to a coin dealer for several hundred dollars; the story is picked up by a news association and is carried in the daily press from coast to coast—or the Treasury Department throws into circulation through the banking system several million silver dollars (as it did in the mid-1960's)—coins which had lain in the vaults for a generation. undisturbed, still in bright, newly minted condition and containing many dates considered rare. The story is headlined in a great eastern daily and almost at once the switchboard of a leading coin dealer is clogged with thousands of incoming phone calls—urgent inquiries from both buyers and sellers—or a banker leaves a map with his will, leading to a hoard of gold coins buried on his estate. The government seizes the coins, you read about it, you hear about it, and you wait to see if the heirs will ever get the coins. The story has a happy ending; they do. The government says that all gold coins may be freely bought and sold or otherwise traded in.

On the other hand, you may have heard some tales about coins that are not quite authentic. You cannot find a 1913 Liberty Head Nickel, because only five pieces were minted and all are accounted for in known collections; and the likelihood of finding an 1804 Silver Dollar or a 5 Dollar gold piece of 1822, or a Brasher Doubloon challenges the laws of probability; no U.S. coin has ever been called in because of a defect in the design; the Columbian Half Dollar of 1892 is not worth $10,000.00, as was once mistakenly reported.

The so-called fabulous coins do, of course, exist, but they are not easily to be found or had. The great rarities of U.S. coinage—the pieces that bring many hundreds of dollars—were recognized as rare and valuable almost immediately after striking and they have been jealously guarded ever since by the intelligent, well-informed and alert collectors in each generation. Therefore, if one does come across an 1827 Quarter, or an 1838-O Half-Dollar, or an 1804 Silver Dollar; if you should have a 3 Dollar gold piece of 1875 or a 4 Dollar gold piece of 1880 or a 5 Dollar gold piece of 1815, then it is most likely that these coins were originally purchased as rare collectors' items for large sums of money, and have come from a highly regarded coin collection, rather than from the accumulated small change of bygone days.

But instead of a few dozen legendary pieces, we still have the main output of U.S. coinage for our field of activity, containing, as it does, multitudes of coins with cash premium values ranging from the modest to the substantial. It is the search for, and the recognition of these coins that is occupying so many millions of Americans today, for pleasure as a pastime or for business as a profession. It is for them and for you that this volume has been created, and in our attempt to make it the finest and most useful coin book of its kind in existence it has of necessity become

A COMPLETE CATALOGUE OF U.S. COINS

from 1652 to date, including the pre-revolutionary Colonial coinage as well as the Pioneer gold coinage struck after the California gold rush at the various Territorial Mints.

We have thus accounted for all the "hard money" that has ever been issued in this country; but what of our paper money? The first U.S. Government notes were issued in 1861 and since then many rare and valuable notes have been produced, including some of quite recent years. These are just as much sought after and collected as are coins and for many years now currency for collectors has assumed an importance equal to that of coins.

We have therefore decided to present the subject of American monetary issues in its entirety and accordingly you will find in this book, as an adjunct to the coin listing, a companion catalogue of

ALL TYPES AND SERIES OF U.S. PAPER MONEY

ALL TYPES OF CONFEDERATE PAPER MONEY

from 1861 to the present day and including (a) the early large size notes, (b) the later or present size notes, (c) Fractional Currency issues–the 3, 5, 10, 15, 25 and 50 Cent notes which circulated as U.S. paper money in the 1860's and 1870's, and which are still legal tender, (d) Confederate Money from the 50 Cent note to the 1000 Dollar note.

The tabular arrangement used in cataloguing the paper money has been designed for efficient use and the information given is both concise and complete, so that even without illustrations, you will be able to locate and identify any note without any confusion.

The concluding section of this book is devoted to the coinage of our neighbors to the north, with whom we share such a long common border. As with the U.S. coinage, we have aimed for thorough coverage and in these pages you will also find a complete catalogue of

THE COINS OF CANADA AND NEWFOUNDLAND

together with those of New Brunswick, Nova Scotia, Prince Edward Island and British Columbia. The Canadian series begins in 1858 when the first, true coins on the Dollar or Decimal standard were issued.

The inclusion of the Canadian series in this catalogue is not an afterthought but is rather dictated by the existing necessity for this information, since the Canadian issues rank next in popularity to U.S. coins. Canadian coins are now considered as important as our domestic coins, and in some sections of the country they form the major part of numismatic activity. A glance at the catalogue will reveal many coins with high premium values and an active interest in the coinage of British North America can prove to be a rewarding experience.

With the inclusion of the Canadian series in this volume the publishers believe this to be

A UNIQUE BOOK

in the annals of numismatic literature, since never before has so much varied and useful information been offered in a single, low-priced, convenient book. For example, until now there has never been a listing in the same book of the premium values of paper money together with coins. The premium books of the past have rarely had listings with any completeness of both Colonial coins and Pioneer gold coins.

It is thus believed that by the proper reference to this book, one should be able to evaluate any coin of American origin, any type of U.S. or Confederate paper money and any coin in the British North American series. It is important at this point to attempt an answer to the question

WHAT MAKES A COIN VALUABLE?

a perplexing and sometimes vexing question. At the outset let it be said that mere age alone has nothing to do with establishing the value of a coin. Many persons mistakenly regard the figure 100 with especial reverence, thinking that the age of 100 years or more automatically confers a special value on a coin. This is simply not so, as an analysis of the coin valuations will reveal. For example, the 1794 Cent commands a premium of $50.00, but the 1877 Cent brings $125.00. A bronze coin of ancient Greece from about 350 B.C. can be bought for about $20.00; a silver coin of Rome from about 200 A.D. for about $40.00; an English Shilling of Queen Elizabeth dated 1587 for about $15.00— and so on—yet a *1923-D Quarter–only 70 years old at the present writing has a premium value of $45.00.*

There are actually three factors which combine to determine the cash premium value of any coin, namely, rarity, demand and condition. The first of these

RARITY

is the most important, since without rarity, the other two factors are only of minor significance. A coin becomes rare out of various circumstances; it may be struck in much fewer numbers than is normal for a contemporary coin of that type (witness the 1877 Cent, the 1931-S Cent, the 1885 Nickel, the 1916-D Dime, the 1901-S Quarter); or it may be a coin of a type struck in only one year (witness the 1793 Half-Cent, the 1796 Quarter, the 1808 Quarter Eagle, the 1907 Double Eagle with Roman numerals); or it may be a coin struck in relatively large numbers for the period but of which only a very few have survived (witness the 1802 Half-Dime, the 1873-CC Dime, the 1876-CC 20 Cent piece, the 1822 Half-Eagle); or it may be one of the fabled pieces of which so few were struck to begin with that it became a great rarity on the day of minting (witness the 1913 Liberty Head Nickel, the 1894-S Dime, the 1804 Silver dollar, the 1885 Trade dollar, any proof coin before 1858); or, as is also likely, the rarity may be determined by the condition of the coin. In these days when millions of collectors are competing for and buying up the choicest specimens, coins which may be very common in used or circulated condition have become quite rare in new or uncirculated condition (witness the entire series of 10, 25 and 50 cent pieces from 1892 to 1933, all Liberty Head nickels, most Indian Head cents, early Lincoln cents with mint marks, etc.). In fact almost any uncirculated coin before about 1930 is now considered scarce in one degree or another.

Assuming then that a given coin is of some rarity, another factor that determines its value is

DEMAND

which is both judge and jury and your only true indicator of the coin's popularity in the numismatic market place. No matter how rare a coin may be, it cannot be easily sold for a price commensurate with its rarity, unless there is a demand for it by collectors. This demand manifests itself to the professional coin dealer through his customers. Repeated requests for a coin not in his stock automatically create a demand for that coin, and if he wishes to stay in business, he must sooner or later buy it. The ultimate demand is thus created by the ultimate consumer, the collector himself, but the large amounts of cash that support the numismatic market are furnished by the professional coin dealers, who thus perform an essential service for both seller and buyer.

It is obvious that all coins cannot be equally in demand at all times; that is why so many coins appear to have a value disproportionately high or low in relation to their rarity. As mentioned above, demand, and hence value, is created by the mass of collectors who are subject to all sorts of collecting impulses. Hence there are fashions, changes of taste and recurrent cycles in coin collecting, as there are in other cultural pursuits. One year Roosevelt Dimes may be the rage; the next year Franklin Half-Dollars; then it may be Proof Sets or Commemoratives or rolls of coins.

But out of all the welter of intense numismatic activity, one trend remains constant through the years—the lower the denomination of the coin, the greater the demand. Hence the King of American coins is the Cent. There are millions more who collect cents—Lincoln and Indian—than any other coins; many more who collect dimes than quarters; many more who collect silver dollars than 5 dollar gold pieces; and many more who collect 20 dollar gold pieces than 50 Dollar bills.

One example selected out of many will show how demand is uncompromising and inexorable in determining coin values. The 1914-D Lincoln cent with a coinage of 1,193,000 pieces has a listed premium value of $40.00, but the 1914-S Quarter with a much smaller coinage of 264,000 pieces lists at only $22.50; compare both with the Cent of 1814—a hundred years earlier—which has a coinage of 357,800 pieces and a listed value of $13.00. Obviously, the 1914-D Cent will tend to keep increasing in value, whereas the other two coins will tend to remain about as they are—unless there is a radical change in collecting habits.

An analysis of the material in this book will reveal much interesting and some surprising data about our coins and their values. Fortunately for numismatics, there are now so many collectors clamoring for all types of coins and there is so much nationwide interest in coin and currency collecting, that one will find a ready sale for almost any American coin, providing always, of course, that it is in suitable

CONDITION

for collecting purposes, since condition, or the state of preservation, is the third factor that helps determine the value of a coin.

Regarded purely as objects of the past (a Greek urn, a Flemish tapestry, a Colt firearm), coins are desired by collectors in the finest condition in which they can be found, within a given price range. Some can afford the finest pieces, others only the average ones. Perhaps this love of new, beautiful coins goes back to our childhood. How pleased we were to be given a new, shiny coin in our change and how reluctant we were to spend it! The true collector among us did not spend it but put it away—if he could afford it—and when found again many years later, it would still be in new condition and by then it would have gained something else-numismatic value.

In this respect a new coin may be likened to a beautiful woman in the full bloom of her youth—lustrous, desirable and admired by all; but as she circulates through the days and years of her life, subtle changes occur in her appearance and after a certain length of time she bears little resemblance to the thing she once was; only her identity is the same; but if only she were the Sleeping Beauty of the fable, she would be found one hundred years later, still lustrous, desirable and admired by all. Coins have become the true sleeping beauties of our generation and there are many such waiting to be restored to life by the diligent prince charmings who will discover them in their "piggy" banks, attics, family souvenirs, bank vaults, or among long-forgotten, unused possessions.

The condition of a very rare coin is not so important a factor in value as it is of a more common coin. The rare piece would be valuable in its own right and the difference in value between the best and poorest condition would not be too great. Some series of coins tend to exist in choice condition, others in poor condition. For example, most modern silver coins exist in well preserved, brilliant condition and there is not much difference in value between an average used piece and a new one. (From about 50 cents to $1.00 for a common silver Washington Quarter.) Early Large Cents, on the other hand, exist mostly in quite worn condition and new pieces are very rare indeed (from about $100.00 to $2,000.00 for the Large Cent of 1795). Among other recent coins for example the 1927-S Quarter in average used condition has a premium listing of only $3.00 but a new or uncirculated specimen can easily be sold for $1,500.00 because it is so very rare in this choice condition. Similarly, from used to new, the 1926-S Nickel ranges from $2.75 to about $400.00, the 1921 Half-Dollar from $24.00 to about $2,000.00, the 1927-D Dime from $1.00 to about $250.00; but the 1909-S-VDB Cent, which is a rare coin in any condition, has a narrow range of values, and a used piece brings about $150.00, a new piece about $300.00.

It is thus evident that condition is intimately tied to rarity and hence to demand, and it is these three factors operating together in various proportions that determine the price at which a coin can be sold at a given time in a given place.

The condition of a coin is usually denoted by a degree of fineness. (Please note that the numismatic meaning of the word "fine" is quite different from its literary meaning, as will be seen below.) The standard terms used in grading the condition of coins, their abbreviations, and what the terms mean are as follows:

—

PROOF or PR. The ultimate condition of coins, since proof coins are struck purely for collectors and not for circulation. The greatest care is lavished in their production so that they will emerge as supreme examples of the art of coinage. A premium over face value has always been charged by the Mint for its proof coins. The coins are struck from scientifically polished dies and metal blanks, and the resultant proof coins are easily recognized by their unusual brilliance. They shine like no other coins you have ever seen, because the surface of a proof coin is like that of a spotless mirror. You can actually see yourself in one of these coins.

UNCIRCULATED or UNC. This denotes a coin in new or unused condition and Unc. coins are usually in the same brilliant condition as when they left the mint. That shiny coin you sometimes get from your bank is considered an Unc. coin if you are the first person to whom this coin has been paid out in the normal course of coin distribution from government mint to local bank via the Federal Reserve System. As soon as you have put your finger marks on the coin and let it jingle in your pocket with other coins for any length of time, it is no longer considered Unc. in the true sense of the word.

EXTREMELY FINE or EF. This denotes a coin which has been in circulation so little, that it shows only the slightest sign of wear or use. For the most part, an EF coin still retains the lustre or mint bloom of an Unc. piece. Actually many EF coins are truly Unc. pieces which have been poorly handled through the years, so that they now show slight friction, minor abrasions or other unimportant blemishes.

VERY FINE or VF. A coin described as VF will generally have been in circulation a relatively short time. It will certainly show evidence of use such as loss of lustre, wear on the highest struck portions, and a proportionate amount of small surface markings which, however, do not detract from the over-all choiceness of true VF quality. Every detail of lettering and design that was originally impressed into the coin will be boldly visible. In general, a coin taken out of your change at random, that is from one to two years old, will tend to be in VF condition.

FINE or F. A fine coin has begun to show signs of more obvious circulation and can best be recognized by the letters and numerals appearing on it. By now they have become somewhat thick and blurry from the constant soft friction of circulation. All of the larger letters will be fully visible but the smaller ones may have begun to fade in a coin rated as fine. If the coin is silver, the reeding or milling on the edge will have begun to lose its character, and is approaching the point when it will vanish from the coin altogether, leaving it with a smooth edge. A truly fine coin makes an overall pleasing impression on the eye, as the amount of circulation is nicely and evenly distributed over its entire surface, but is still not severe enough to give the coin a shopworn appearance.

VERY GOOD and GOOD or VG and G. These two terms are all-embracing in scope because they accurately describe the condition of most of the millions of non-current coins now in existence. (By non-current we mean all types of coins except those presently being struck.) These terms are used singly as VG and G or sometimes together as G-VG. Coins in either of these two conditions (between which there is only a minor difference in value) are the general, run-of-the-mill, circulated coins found everywhere. They have spent long, faithful years in the service of their country and they look it. The reason so very many of our older type coins are found in this condition is that there were few coin collectors in the old days. Consequently most coins got into circulation and stayed there for many years, passing routinely into the government melting pot or casually into a private holding.

G and VG coins present a well-worn appearance and are in a more advanced state of circulation than fine coins. Most of the larger letters will have shrunk somewhat from the creeping paralysis of circulation, moving from the outer edge of the coin to the center. The smaller lettering may have disappeared altogether, such as the word "Liberty" which appears on the head band of a Liberty-head coin or on an Indian Head Cent. But such coins are still recognizable for what they are; you can easily read the date, the denomination, the main legends and the mint mark, if any. Just as they are the most common, so are they the most widely collected, because they represent decent, collectible coins at moderate prices, the appeal thus being to the great mass of collectors. **In this book, for example, the valuations are based on the coins being in G-VG condition, except as noted elsewhere in the catalogue proper.**

FAIR and POOR. These two terms (no standard abbreviations) are used for coins in the lowest possible condition. Such coins are so badly worn or have such defects, that they are barely recognizable and hence are called "space fillers." They will do in a collection simply because better ones cannot be found or may cost too much. Only very rare coins would command a premium in fair or poor condition. Such coins might be a 1793 Half Cent or Cent, a 1794 Dollar, or 1796 Half Cent, Quarter, or Half-Dollar, etc. Fair and poor coins present an appearance which some have described as miserable. Most of the design and lettering are gone and so little remains on the coin that sometimes only experienced numismatic deduction can properly attribute it.

Sometimes coins will be found that cannot properly be described by any of the above conditions because they have been mutilated in various ways or are false. **Such coins are of no numismatic value and command no premium.** If genuine, they are worth only their face amount, but if a hole has been drilled into any coin it has lost even its face value, since the government will not redeem such a coin. Some of these various mutilations, defects or deceptions are described as follows:—

HOLED. A coin with a hole drilled completely through it.

PLUGGED HOLE. A holed coin in which the hole has been filled in with some metal to reduce the ugliness of the coin.

LOOPED. A coin with a loop attached to the edge by solder, enabling it to be attached to a chain. This is most common in gold coins.

LOOP REMOVED. A coin from which a loop has been removed by breaking or sawing it off. The edge of the coin will usually reveal evidence of a former loop.

GILDED. Any coin which has been gold plated.

NAMES and INITIALS. These will sometimes be found scratched, engraved or stamped on coins. Only in the case of a great rarity would a coin thus mutilated command a premium.

ELECTROTYPE. A false coin made by making impressions of a genuine coin on a thin shell of the same metal. The Obv. and Rev. are on different shells, which are then joined after filling them with a cheap alloy to give them weight. A thin line running around the edge will usually identify an electrotype, as well as the fact that it will not have the true ring of a genuine coin.

CAST. A false coin made by making a cast from a genuine coin. Casts can generally be identified by a rough, mottled surface.

ALTERED DATE. A false coin made by changing the date on a genuine coin to another date of much greater rarity and value. Some altered date coins are very dimicult to detect and hence dangerous, bearing in mind that the coin itself is genuine. A strong magnifier will generally discover this deception.

MINT MARK ADDED OR REMOVED. Similar in principle to altered date coins, but in this case, the mint mark, not the date, has been tampered with. A mint mark may be added to a coin or removed from it, in order to make it more valuable. As with altered date coins, a strong magnifier should be used on a suspected piece.

POLISHED COINS. Although not mutilated, coins which have been polished to a high shine by cleaning powders, polishing creams, or other abrasives lose a great deal of their premium value, even if in otherwise choice condition. Coins should be left in the same state of preservation as when found, and no attempt should be made to clean or polish them, no matter how dirty they may appear.

TOKENS—CALIFORNIA GOLD PIECES

Sometimes copper or nickel pieces will be found which appear to be U.S. coins and yet cannot be located in this book, which is complete insofar as U.S. coinage is concerned. Such pieces will no doubt turn out to be privately struck tokens of the 19th century. Enormous amounts of these were made during the late 1830's and early 1860's. In both cases the tokens were issued to relieve shortages of small change and they actually circulated as 1 Cent pieces; the early pieces being the size of large Cents and called "Hard Times Tokens"; the later pieces being the size of small Cents and called "Civil War Cents." Such tokens generally have a cash premium value of from $1.00 to $2.00 each.

Other coins which appear to be U.S. pieces are the so-called California gold coins. Like the tokens described above, they are not really coins but private issues; in neither case were they struck under authority of the U.S. Government, nor did they emanate from any government mint.

These California gold pieces—also called charms—exist in denominations of ¼, ½ and 1 Dollar; they may be round or they may be octagonal in shape; they are quite tiny and very thin and they may, or may not, be of gold; some of them have been restruck in recent years.

They were first made in the middle of the 19th Century, ostensibly to augment the gold coins then in circulation out West. It is doubtful if they ever served that purpose, because their minute size and insubstantial weight must have made them impossible to handle with any assurance of safety.

Those pieces are considered to be the original issues which are struck in genuine gold and have the word, "Dollar" or "Dol" as part of the denomination. In this case they have a value ranging from about $25.00 to $50.00. Any other pieces are worth considerably less.

APPRAISING AND SELLING YOUR COINS

If you have any U.S. coins or currency for sale or any Canadian coins, it would be prudent to acquaint yourself with the contents of this book, so that you can be better informed and be guided accordingly.

This book has been so prepared that by proper reference to the catalogue section as well as to this Preface and to the General Information which follows, you will be able to appraise your coins yourself and estimate their cash value with a fair degree of accuracy. The following points should be borne in mind when appraising and selling your coins:—

PRICE. **The cash premium values in this book reflect the approximate prices that established, professional coin dealers will pay for material. These values, which are averages, have been arrived at by a careful study of many years duration of market conditions and buying trends from coast to coast. Since the valuations are averages, the price actually offered may vary from the published values.**

SUPPLY. Sometimes a dealer will not wish to buy certain coins—even high-premium pieces—because he has an ample supply of them at the time of offer. In this respect he is like any other merchant who has to exercise a certain amount of inventory control to keep him from getting unhealthily overstocked in any one item.

DEMAND. On the other hand, if your coins are popular issues and continually in demand, the dealer will be tempted to buy them even though he has an ample stock. In this case, he is taking a calculated risk, based on his experiences and judgment, and he is gambling either that the demand will continue strong or that the coins will enhance in value.

RARITY. In general, the higher the premium value of the coin, the easier it will be to sell. A coin with a value very much above its face value, or very much above the average for that type, will tend to be a scarce coin in short supply and hence in demand.

CONDITION. The values in this book are based on the condition in which the coins are most frequently found, namely, good to very good, as has been proven by experience. If your coins are in much choicer condition they will command a higher price than listed; if in inferior condition either a lower price, or no premium at all, will prevail. In some cases, as will be noted in the catalogue, the valuations are for uncirculated or proof specimens. In the case of all gold coins the valuations are for specimens in choice, well preserved condition, ranging from extremely fine to uncirculated.

CLEANING. As noted earlier, coins should be left in the same condition as when found. No attempt should be made to alter their appearance by cleaning or polishing.

COIN DEALERS. Coins and currency should be offered to professional coin dealers established in a regular place of business. For a list of the coin dealers in any community, consult the local classified telephone directory under the heading "Coin Dealers," or those Sunday newspapers that have a Stamp and Coin section and carry the advertising of coin dealers. The material you have may be brought to them in person or it may be shipped in for their inspection and offer, or a list of it may be sent by mail to see if they are interested.

MINT AND MINT MARKS—ABBREVIATIONS

The capital letters you will see after certain dates represent mint marks. They appear in this manner: 1853-O, 1878-S, 1890-CC, etc. The actual spot on the coin where the mint mark may be found is indicated clearly in the catalogue, before the listing of each type of coin. The letters and the mints they represent are as follows (please remember that coins struck at the Philadelphia mint do not have a mint mark except as noted below):—

C—Charlotte, N.C. On gold coins only from 1838–1861.

CC—Carson City, Nev. On gold and silver coins from 1870–1893.

D—Dahlonega, Ga. On gold coins only from 1838–1861.

D—Denver, Colo. On all coins from 1906–1964, 1968 to date.

O—New Orleans, La. On gold and silver coins from 1838–1909.

P—Philadelphia, Pa. On nickels from 1942–1945. On Anthony dollars from 1979 to date. On nickels, dimes, quarters and half dollars from 1980 to date.

S—San Francisco, Calif. On all coins from 1854–1955, 1968 to date.

W—West Point, N.Y. On certain modern commemoratives.

CANADIAN ISSUES

H—Heaton Mint in Birmingham, England.

C—Ottawa Mint in Canada.

No mint mark—Before 1908, London and after 1908, Ottawa.

Abbreviations for the condition of coins are given under the heading "Condition" (see above). Other abbreviations used are:

OBV.—Obverse or the "head" side of a coin.

REV.—Reverse or the "tail" side of a coin.

ARR.—Arrows, as on certain silver coins from 1853–1855 and 1873–1874.

In the General Information, which follows, you will find important data on various coins.

General Information

(Notes and comments on various coins, giving more specific or detailed information than is to be found in the catalogue proper.)

COLONIAL AND STATE COINAGE

Many of these coins are so rare, that forgeries have been created. There are various types of these forgeries, such as electrotypes, casts and struck copies. The last type is especially difficult to recognize since the forged piece is struck from an actual die manufactured for that purpose. In general, any very rare Colonial coin in really first class condition should be suspected of being a forgery or other type of facsimile, and all such pieces should be authenticated.

CAROLINA ELEPHANT TOKEN COINAGE. A very rare variety has the spelling "Proprieters." Forgeries exist.

CONNECTICUT. Higley Token Coinage. Forgeries exist. There is also a unique variety in which a wheel appears on the Rev. In the State Coinage, there are very many minor varieties in the appearance of the bust and in the spelling of the legends.

MARYLAND. Forgeries exist of the Lord Baltimore Penny, which is a very rare coin. The head on the 3 Pence piece of Standish Barry is reputed to be that of Washington. This coin has the date as "July 4, 90."

MASSACHUSETTS. Forgeries exist of the NE coinage and of the Oak Tree and Pine Tree issues. In the State Coinage there is a rare variety of the 1787 Cent in which the eagle holds the bundle of arrows in the right talon, rather than in the left one.

NEW ENGLAND COINAGE. The Elephant Half Penny of 1694 is similar in design to the Carolina Half Penny of 1694. The New England piece, however, is extremely rare and forgeries exist.

NEW HAMPSHIRE. Forgeries are known of the 1776 Cent.

NEW JERSEY. The St. Patrick coins, sometimes attributed to New Jersey, will be found in Part Two, since they bear nothing on them to identify them with New Jersey. A scarce variety of the 1788 Cent shows the horse's head facing to the left.

NEW YORK. Forgeries exist of the Cents of Gov. Clinton, of the "Non VI . . ." type, of the Indian type and of the Excelsior type. A unique specimen is known of a New York Cent which shows the head of George III on one side and a standing Indian on the other. There are several varieties of the 1787 Cent with laureate male bust. These varieties are called "Nova Eboracs" (New Yorks). The bust may differ in size or the seated figure may face either to right or left.

UNITED STATES OF AMERICA. The 1792 coinage of the U.S. Mint has traditionally been catalogued with Colonial Coins, the whole forming the subject of Early American Coins. The 1792 coins were experimental and all are very rare and seldom met with, except for the Half Disme. Regular U.S. coinage began in 1793. (The illustration of the 1792 Cent with silver center does not show the silver center.)

On the other hand, the Fugio Cents of 1787 were the first coins issued under the authority of the United States Goverment and were reportedly struck at New Haven. These actually circulated and are far commoner than the 1792 issues.

CONFEDERATIO COINAGE. Forgeries exist of the 1785 Cent.

THE CONTINENTAL DOLLAR. On some varieties, the word is spelled as "Curency." Forgeries and imitations are known.

NOVA CONSTELLATIO—IMMUNE COLUMBIA COINAGE. The "U.S." that appears on the Rev. of the 1783–1786 Cents may be either in block letters or in a script monogram. On some varieties the word is spelled as "Constelatio." Forgeries are known of the 1785 Cents inscribed "Immune Columbia."

THE TRIANGLE TOKEN. This piece has sometimes been called a Kentucky Cent, only because "K" appears at the top of the triangle of 15 rosettes, each bearing an initial of one of the 15 states. Otherwise, this coin does not bear the name of a specific colony.

GEORGE WASHINGTON COINS AND TOKENS. Forgeries are known of most valuable pieces including the 1792 Half Dollars.

UNITED STATES COINS

HALF CENTS. Various type forgeries are known of 1793 and 1796 and electrotype forgeries mainly of 1831, 1836, 1852, and 1840–1848 inclusive.

1797. A rare variety has lettering on the edge.

1808. A scarce variety shows the last 8 struck over a 7.

LARGE CENTS. 1793. All three major varieties of this date have been forged, mainly by electrotyping. "America" on the Chain type sometimes appears as "Ameri"; the wreath type has either lettering on the edge or vines and bars, and there is an extremely rare variety with a strawberry sprig under the head rather than a 3-leaf sprig.

1797. A scarce variety has a stemless wreath on the Rev.

1798. A scarce variety has the Rev. typical of 1796 Cents.

1799. This coin has been extensively forged by altering the date of another Large Cent of similar type to read 1799.

1801. A scarce variety has three errors in the design; there is but one stem to the wreath; the fraction appears as 1/000 and "United" as "llnited."

1804. This coin too has been forged by altering the date of another coin.

1815. Cents have been struck in every year from 1793 to date except 1815. In order to maintain an unbroken continuity of years, some collectors have altered other cents to read "1815." An 1815 Cent is therefore a fantasy created by self delusion.

1839. A rare variety shows the 9 struck over a 6.

FLYING EAGLE CENTS. 1856. More forgeries must exist of this date than of any other U.S. coin. Most of these forgeries are altered dates, which are clearly visible under a strong magnifier; 1858 Cents have been used most often for this alteration, the last 8 being converted into a 6.

INDIAN HEAD CENTS. 1864-L. The L appears as a quite small letter at the end of the ribbon as it trails off the feather head dress on the Indian head.

LINCOLN HEAD CENTS. 1909-VDB. The VDB appears as three small letters at the extreme bottom of the Rev. They indicate the initials of the designer, Mr. Victor D. Brenner.

1914-D. This coin has recently been forged by alteration. A "D" has been added to a plain 1914 Cent or a D mint marked coin ending in a 4 has been changed to 1914.

2 CENT PIECES. 1864 Small Motto. This refers to "In God We Trust." The quickest way to distinguish the small letters in the motto from the large ones in the Large Motto type is to look at the letter D in God. In the Small Motto the D is quite rounded: in the large motto it is narrow and oval.

BUFFALO NICKELS. A scarce variety of 1918-D shows the 8 struck over a 7. The 3-legged buffalo of 1937-D shows the buffalo standing on only three legs, the result of a die defect obliterating the fourth leg.

HALF DIMES. 1796. A rare variety shows the 6 struck over the 5 of 1795.

1872-S. The mint mark may be either within or below the wreath.

DIMES. 1811. All coins are struck over 1809.

1823. All coins are struck over 1822.

1824. All coins are struck over 1822.

1873-CC. Only one specimen is known without arrows at the date.

1875. The S and CC mint marks may be either within or below the wreath.

1942/1. A scarce variety exists on which the 2 is struck over the 1 of 1941.

QUARTERS. 1822. A rare variety shows the 25c on the Rev. struck over 50c.

1823. All coins are struck over 1822.

1825. All coins are struck over other dates.

1828. A rare variety shows the 25c struck over 50c.

1842. A rare variety has a small date and exists in proof condition only.

1853/2. All coins are struck over 1852, and are without arrows. This coin has been forged by changing the last 8 of an 1858 into a 3.

1918-S/17. A scarce variety shows the 8 struck over the 7 of a 1917-S.

HALF DOLLARS. 1795. A rare variety shows a stem with three leaves, rather than two, on the upper part of the branch under each wing of the eagle.

1805-1836. Coins of these years are rich in varieties. There are overdates, small and large dates, small and large letters, etc.

1842-O. A rare variety exists with the date much smaller in size.

1846. A rare variety shows the 6 struck over another 6 at right angles to it.

1846-O. A scarce variety shows the date in much taller numerals.

1847. A rare variety shows the 7 struck over the 6 of an 1846.

1853-O without arrows or rays. This great rarity has been forged by altering the last 8 of an 1858-O to a 3.

1917. The mint marks may appear on the Obv. under the motto or on the Rev. to the left of "Half Dollar."

SILVER DOLLARS. 1797. A rare variety has the Rev. legend in smaller letters with a 9 × 7 arrangement of the stars on the Obv.

1895. This rare coin, which exists in proof condition only, has been forged by removing the mint marks on an 1895-O or 1895-S.

UNITED STATES PROOF SETS

The prices of proof sets are subject to some very sudden changes, either upward or downward. This is caused by the private accumulation of large amounts of sets and the resultant speculation therein.

U.S. SILVER COMMEMORATIVE COINS

GRANT 1922*. This coin has been forged by adding a star to an ordinary Grant Half Dollar. All Grant coins with star should be authenticated.

BOONE, 1934–1938. The small 1934 appears on all issues beginning with 1935. It will be found to the right of the standing figure on the Rev.

U.S. GOLD COMMEMORATIVE COINS

LEWIS AND CLARK ISSUE. The Gold Dollars of this issue tended to be used as jewelry. All specimens should be examined for evidence of loop removed or solder remains.

UNITED STATES GOLD COINS

1 DOLLAR. A minor variety appears in the 1849 coinage. The wreath on the Rev. may form a full circle or an open circle.

2½ DOLLARS. 1802. All coins are struck over 1801.

1806. All coins are struck over 1804 or 1805.

1824. All coins are struck over 1821.

1826. All coins are struck over 1825.

1841. This coin has been forged by removing the mint marks from 1841-C or 1841-D coins.

1854-S. This coin has been forged by adding an S mint mark to an 1854 coin of the Philadelphia Mint.

1863. This coin exists in proof condition only, but forgeries have been made by removing the S from 1863-S coins.

3 DOLLARS. 1873 and 1878. These dates should always be looked at under a magnifier. Many persons have accidentally misread these dates because the 3 and the 8 tend to look similar at first glance.

4 DOLLARS. These pieces should always be authenticated as being of gold. Genuine specimens struck from these dies in minor metals as patterns, have sometimes been gold plated as a deception or as an act of self-delusion.

5 DOLLARS. 1795, 1797 and 1798. These three dates each exist in two distinct types; please see the catalogue for proper attribution.

1802. All coins are struck over 1801.

1803. All coins are struck over 1802.

1825. All coins are struck over 1821 or 1824.

1807 and 1834. These two dates each exist in two distinct types.

1854-S. This very rare coin should always be verified as not being an 1854 Philadelphia coin to which an S has later been added.

1887. This coin was struck only in proof condition but forgeries have been made by removing the S mint mark from an 1887-S.

1909-O. This coin should be carefully examined to verify that the mint mark is genuine, or if genuine, that the O is not being mis-read for a D, since these mint marks are usually quite weak.

10 DOLLARS. 1797. This date exists in two distinct types.

1858. Forgeries have been created by removing the mint marks from 1858-O or 1858-S coins.

1907, 1908. These dates exist in more than one distinct type.

20 DOLLARS. 1861 and 1861-S. Each of these two coins exists as a great rarity when the Rev. design is the Paquet type. This type can be identified by the much taller letters in the legend.

1907, 1908. These dates exist in more than one distinct type.

All rare coins of the Philadelphia Mint should be examined for evidence of removed mint marks.

Rare date issues of the period 1908–1932 are subject to sudden price changes, as large amounts tend to be found unexpectedly from time to time.

In recent years, counterfeit coins, struck in gold, have appeared in all denominations, rare as well as common dates.

PIONEER GOLD COINS

The valuations are for coins in average VG-F condition. Really choice pieces are very rare and would command higher prices. If several varieties exist of a given coin, the valuation is for the commonest one.

NORRIS, GRIEG & NORRIS. A 5 Dollar piece has recently been discovered issued at Stockton rather than San Francisco.

TEMPLETON REID. The only known specimen of the 25 Dollar piece of 1849 was stolen in 1858 from the U.S. Mint collection and has never been recovered.

UNITED STATES PAPER MONEY

CONFEDERATE PAPER MONEY

The valuations given for the large size notes and Fractional Currency are for specimens in presentable, used condition (fine to very fine) and not giving a dirty, shopworn appearance. Notes which are torn, thin from use, very badly wrinkled or generally unattractive, would command a smaller premium than listed or none at all, since currency is collected mainly for the beauty and eye appeal inherent in well preserved specimens. Notes which are in new or unused condition would naturally be purchased at higher prices than listed.

Small size or present day notes, on the other hand, are valued in new condition only. Since the notes are recent and more readily available, they are not generally wanted in used condition.

Those who are interested in a fully illustrated book on U.S. paper money are referred to the standard work on this subject, "Paper Money of the United States" by Robert Friedberg. This complete and definitive volume illustrates front and back of every type of paper money ever issued from the 3 Cent note to the 10,000 Dollar note and from the first year of issue in 1861 to the present day. In addition, all varieties of seals and signatures are listed with collectors' valuations. "Paper Money of the United States" is available at almost any coin dealer or you may write for information to the publishers of this book.

There are many varieties of currency, formed by differences in the seals, signatures, series letters, etc., and in all cases, the valuations are for the commoner varieties.

THE COINAGE OF BRITISH NORTH AMERICA

This series begins with the Canadian issues of 1858, which were the first true coins based on the Canadian Dollar consisting of 100 Cents. Prior to 1858, the coinage in use consisted of a miscellaneous variety of copper tokens based on the English Pound. There are hundreds of varieties of these Penny and Half Penny tokens, most of them of only small value (from about .10 to .50) and they are omitted from this book because they are not considered as coins.

Following the introduction of Canadian coins in 1858, the first coins of Newfoundland were issued in 1865, and of Nova Scotia and New Brunswick in

1861. The only issue of Prince Edward Island was a 1 Cent piece in 1871 and of British Columbia a 10 and 20 Dollar gold piece in 1862. These gold coins, however, were not placed in circulation because of opposition from England.

As with the U.S. coins, the valuations for Canadian coins are based on G-VG condition except where otherwise stated.

In 1936 a small dot was placed under the date on some of the 1, 10 and 25 Cent pieces struck in that year. 25 Cent pieces with the dot are somewhat scarce, but the 1 and 10 Cent pieces are very rare.

The maple leaf on part of the 1947 coinage of all denominations may be found as a quite small symbol to the immediate right of the date.

CANADIAN COIN VARIETIES. There are some variations from the normal among certain Canadian coins, making them of greater scarcity and value. The most important varieties follow.

1 Cent 1859. Struck over 1858.

1 Cent 1891. With a smaller date than normal.

1 Cent 1936. With dot below date.

5 Cents 1858. With a larger date than normal.

5 Cents 1900. With round O's in date rather than oval.

5 Cents 1902-H. With a smaller H mint mark than normal.

5 Cents 1921. Not a variety but very rare as a coin because most of the 2½ million struck were melted down rather than issued.

10 Cents 1893. With the top part of the 3 rounded rather than flat.

10 Cents 1913. With larger leaves on the Rev. than normal.

10 Cents 1936. With dot below date.

25 Cents 1936. With dot below the wreath under date.

50 Cents 1921. Like the 5 Cents 1921, not a variety but very rare as a coin because most were melted down.

50 Cents 1946. With part of the design extending into the 6.

50 Cents 1947. With maple leaf and a curved 7 pointing to the right, rather than a straight 7 pointing to the left.

1 Dollar 1947. With a pointed 7 rather than a blunt 7 in the date.

Colonial and State Coinage
(1652–1792)

PART ONE

Coins and tokens issued by or for specific colonies or states. These pieces bear either a state name or a device that identifies the state. The valuations below are for coins in used or circulated condition. Bent and holed coins are worthless.

Collectors should be aware that many of the following pieces exist as casts and electrotypes. These are also worthless.

CAROLINA ELEPHANT TOKEN COINAGE

Elephant. Rev. "GOD PRESERVE CAROLINA AND THE LORDS PROPRIETORS 1694," Copper.

Half Penny 1694 . . . . **475.00**

CONNECTICUT
Higley Token Coinage

Deer standing. Rev. Three axes. Copper.

3 Pence 1737 . . . . **2,000.00**

Deer standing. Rev. One large axe. Copper.

3 Pence. No date, 1739 . . . . **2,500.00**

State Coinage

Laureate bust facing right or left. Rev. Female seated. Copper.

1 Cent 1785, 1786, 1787, 1788 . . . . **9.00**

KENTUCKY
Myddelton Token Coinage

Liberty stretching hand out to two children. Rev. Female seated with shield.

1 Cent 1796. Struck in copper **3,200.00**
1 Cent 1796. Struck in silver **2,500.00**

MARYLAND
Cecil Calvert (Lord Baltimore) Coinage

Head of Lord Baltimore. Rev. Crowned shield and Roman numeral. Silver.

1 Shilling. No date (1658) **450.00**
6 Pence. No date (1658) **350.00**
4 Pence. No date (1658) **400.00**

Head of Lord Baltimore. Rev. Two flags over crown. Copper.

1 Penny (Denarium). No date (1658) . . . . **Very Rare**

Annapolis Token Coinage of John Chalmers

Clasped hands in wreath. Rev. Two birds and snake within circle. Silver.

1 Shilling 1783 . . . . **200.00**

Clasped hands. Rev. Circle of rings. Silver. (This coin sold for $24,200 in 1983)

1 Shilling 1783 . . . . **Very Rare**

Long cross. Rev. Wreath. Silver.

6 Pence 1783 . . . . **250.00**

Clasped hands. Rev. Plant in wreath. Silver.

3 Pence 1783 . . . . **175.00**

Baltimore Token Coinage of Standish Barry

Large male head. Rev. Name and value. Silver.

3 Pence 1790 . . . . **750.00**

MASSACHUSETTS
NE (New England) Coinage

NE at top, the rest blank. Rev. Roman numeral for value at top, the rest blank. Silver.

1 Shilling. No date (1652) **2,300.00**
6 Pence. No date (1652) . . . . **Very Rare**
3 Pence. No date (1652) . . . . **Very Rare**

Willow Tree Coinage

A willow tree. Rev. Date and Roman numeral for the value. Silver.

1 Shilling 1652 . . . . **1,500.00**
6 Pence 1652 . . . . **Very Rare**
3 Pence 1652 . . . . **Very Rare**

Oak Tree Coinage

An oak tree. Rev. Date and Roman numeral for the value. Silver.

1 Shilling 1652	**125.00**
6 Pence 1652	**125.00**
3 Pence 1652	**125.00**
2 Pence 1662	**100.00**

Pine Tree Coinage

A pine tree. Rev. Date and Roman numeral for the value. Silver.

1 Shilling 1652. Large size	**125.00**
1 Shilling 1652. Small size	**150.00**
6 Pence 1652	**100.00**
3 Pence 1652	**85.00**

State Coinage

Pine tree. Rev. Female seated on globe. Copper.

1 Cent 1776	**Unique**

Three heads in Janiform position. Rev. Female seated on globe. Copper.

Half Penny 1776 . . . . **Unique**

Indian standing. Rev. Spread eagle. Copper.

1 Cent 1787, 1788 . . . . **15.00**
Half Cent 1787, 1788 . . . . **17.50**

NEW ENGLAND COINAGE
Elephant Token Coinage

Elephant. Rev. "GOD PRESERVE NEW ENGLAND 1694." Copper

Half Penny 1694 . . . . **Very Rare**

Lion Token Coinage

Two lions facing in opposite directions. Rev. "NEW ENGLAND." Copper.

Token coin. No date (1675) **600.00**

NEW HAMPSHIRE

Pine tree. Rev. Harp. Copper.

1 Cent 1776 . . . . **5,500.00**

NEW JERSEY

Horse's head and plow with date below plow. Rev. Shield. Copper.

1 Cent 1786, 1787, 1788 . . . . **15.00**

Horse's head and plow with date to right of plow. Rev. Shield. Copper.

1 Cent 1786 . . . . **15.00**

Head of Washington. Rev. Spread eagle. Copper.

1 Cent. No date (1786) . . . . ——

Head of Washington. Rev. Shield. Copper.

1 Cent. No date (1786) . . . . ——

Liberty holding scales, "Immunis Columbia." Rev. Shield. Copper.

1 Cent 1786 . . . . ——

Spread eagle. Rev. Shield. Copper.

1 Cent 1786 . . . . ——

NEW YORK
State Copper Coinage

Bust of Gov. Clinton. Rev. Shield supported by two figures.

1 Cent 1787 . . . . **1,500.00**

Laureate male bust. Rev. Female seated to right or left.

1 Cent 1787 . . . . **25.00**

Armored bust, "NON VI VIRTUTE VICI." Rev. Liberty holding scales.

1 Cent 1786 . . . . **800.00**

Liberty holding scales, "IMMUNIS COLUMBIA." Rev. Eagle.

1 Cent 1787 . . . . **100.00**

Indian standing. Rev. Eagle on globe.

1 Cent 1787 . . . . **1,350.00**

Indian standing. Rev. Shield supported by two figures.

1 Cent 1787 . . . . **1,000.00**

Shield supported by two figures. Rev. Eagle. The EXCELSIOR cent.

1 Cent 1787 . . . . **275.00**

MISCELLANEOUS TOKEN COINAGE
New Yorke in America Token

Spread eagle. Rev. Two figures under palm tree.

Brass token. No date (1700) **1,000.00**

The Mott Token

Large clock. Rev. Eagle. Copper.

Token 1 Cent 1789 . . . . **25.00**

Talbot, Allum & Lee Token

Liberty standing. Rev. Ship. Copper.

1 Cent 1794, 1795 . . . . **12.00**

RHODE ISLAND

Admiral Howe's flagship. Rev. Group of ships.

Copper token 1778, 1779 . . . . **150.00**

UNITED STATES OF AMERICA
Fugio Cent Coinage

Sundial, radiate sun above, and "MIND YOUR BUSINESS" below.
Rev. Circular chain of thirteen links.

1 Cent 1787 . . . . **30.00**

Early Mint Issues

Liberty head. Rev. Flying eagle.

1 Disme 1792. Silver . . . . **Very Rare**
1 Disme 1792. Copper . . . . **Very Rare**
Half Disme 1792. Silver **700.00**

Liberty head. Rev. Wreath. With silver center plug.

1 Cent 1792 . . . . **Very Rare**

Liberty head. Rev. Wreath. The so called Birch Cent, and much larger than the above cent.

1 Cent 1792 . . . . **Very Rare**

U.S.A. Bar Cent

Monogram of USA. Rev. Thirteen bars. Copper.

1 Cent. No date (1785) **100.00**

VERMONT

Hills over plow. Rev. Radiate eye. Copper.

1 Cent 1785,1786 . . . . **45.00**

Male bust. Rev. Seated female, "IMMUNE COLUMBIA." Copper.

1 Cent 1785 . . . . **550.00**

Male bust to right or left. Rev. Seated female. Copper.

1 Cent 1786, 1787, 1788 . . . . **15.00**

VIRGINIA
Gloucester Token Coinage

Building. Rev. Star. Brass.

1 Shilling 1714 . . . . **Very Rare**

English Royal Coinage

Head of George III. Rev. Arms and date.

1 Shilling 1774. Silver . . . . **Rare**
1 Penny 1773. Copper **2,000.00**
Half penny 1773. Copper **15.00**

PART TWO

Coins and tokens issued for general use in early America and not inscribed with the name of any specific colony or state.

AUCTORI PLEBIS TOKEN COINAGE

Male bust, "AUCTORI PLEBIS." Rev. Seated female. Copper.

1 Cent 1787 . . . . **15.00**

CONFEDERATIO COINAGE

Figure at pedestal holding bow and arrow. Rev. Thirteen stars in radiate circle. Copper.

1 Cent 1785 . . . . **Rare**

THE CONTINENTAL DOLLAR

Sundial with radiate sun above. Rev. The names of the thirteen states inscribed on the links of a circular chain. Many copies exist.

1 Dollar 1776. Struck in pewter **450.00**
1 Dollar 1776. Struck in brass . . . . **Very Rare**
1 Dollar 1776. Struck in silver . . . . **Very Rare**

GEORGE III—IMMUNE COLUMBIA COINAGE

Head of George III. Rev. Liberty holding scales "IMMUNE COLUMBIA." Copper.

1 Cent 1785 . . . . **500.00**

GEORGIUS TRIUMPHO TOKEN COINAGE

Laureate male head. Rev. Liberty standing behind screen of thirteen bars. Copper.

1 Cent token 1783 . . . . **20.00**

NORTH AMERICAN TOKEN

Seated female (Hibernia). Rev. Ship. Copper.

Token coin 1781 . . . . **10.00**

NOVA CONSTELLATIO—IMMUNE COLUMBIA COINAGE

Radiate eye. Rev. "U.S." in wreath. Copper. (The U.S. in either block or script letters)

1 Cent 1783, 1785, 1786 . . . . **15.00**

Radiate eye. Rev. Liberty holding scales, "IMMUNE COLUMBIA."

1 Cent 1785. Copper . . . . **Rare**
1 Cent 1785. Struck in silver . . . . ——

PITT TOKEN COINAGE

Bust of William Pitt. Rev. Ship and "AMERICA." Copper.

Half penny 1766 . . . . **60.00**
1 Farthing 1766 . . . . ——

PLANTATION TOKEN COINAGE

Horseman and titles of James II of England. Rev. Four shields. Pewter.
(This token is sometimes attributed to Florida, but was used in many colonies.)

1/24th Part Real 1688 . . . . **70.00**

ST. PATRICK COINAGE OF MARK NEWBY

(Used Mainly in New Jersey)

St. Patrick standing before throng. Rev. Crowned figure playing harp.

Half Penny. No date (1678). Copper **45.00**

St. Patrick holding cross, snakes in foreground. Rev. Crowned figure playing harp.

1 Farthing. No date (1678). Copper **25.00**
1 Farthing. Same but struck in silver **250.00**

THE TRIANGLE TOKEN

Hand holding scroll. Rev. Triangle formed by fifteen stars, each bearing the initial of a state. K for Kentucky is at top. Copper.

1 Cent. No date (1792) **25.00**

VOCE POPULI—HIBERNIA COINAGE

Male bust. Rev. Seated female and "HIBERNIA." Copper.

Half Penny 1760 . . . . **20.00**
1 Farthing 1760 . . . . **60.00**

WOOD'S COINAGE—HIBERNIA TYPE

Head of George I. Rev. Seated female with harp. Copper.

Half Penny 1722, 1723, 1724 . . . . **10.00**
1 Farthing 1722, 1723, 1724 . . . . **10.00**

WOOD'S COINAGE—ROSA AMERICANA TYPE

Head of George I. Rev. Rose. Copper.

2 Pence 1722, 1723 or no date **30.00**
1 Penny 1722, 1723 . . . . **30.00**
Half Penny 1722, 1723 . . . . **25.00**

PART THREE
GEORGE WASHINGTON COINS AND TOKENS

(All are copper except the Half Dollars of 1792)

Obv: Military bust. "WASHINGTON & INDEPENDENCE." Rev: Liberty seated. "UNITED STATES."

1 Cent 1783 . . . . **20.00**

Obv: Head. "WASHINGTON & INDEPENDENCE." Rev: Liberty seated. "UNITED STATES."

1 Cent 1783 . . . . **20.00**

Obv: Head. "WASHINGTON & INDEPENDENCE." Rev: Wreath. "UNITY STATES OF AMERICA."

1 Cent 1783 . . . . **25.00**

Obv: Military bust. "WASHINGTON." Rev: Same bust. "ONE CENT."

1 Cent. No date (1783) **25.00**

Obv: Bust. "WASHINGTON PRESIDENT." Rev: Large or small eagle, "ONE CENT."

1 Cent 1791 . . . . **65.00**

Obv: Bust. "WASHINGTON PRESIDENT." Rev: Ship. "LIVERPOOL HALFPENNY."

Half Penny 1791 . . . . **300.00**

Obv: Bust. "WASHINGTON PRESIDENT." Rev: Large spread eagle. No legend.

1 Cent 1792 . . . . **Rare**

Obv: Laureate Roman-type head to right. "WASHINGTON PRESIDENT." Rev: Eagle. "CENT."

1 Cent 1792 . . . . **Rare**

Obv: Bust. "WASHINGTON PRESIDENT." Rev: In ten lines, "GENERAL OF THE AMERICAN ARMIES 1775. RESIGNED 1788. PRESIDENT OF THE UNITED STATES 1789."

1 Cent 1792 . . . . **Rare**

Obv: Bust. "GEO. WASHINGTON BORN VIRGINIA FEBRUARY 11, 1732." Rev: In ten lines,
"GENERAL OF THE AMERICAN ARMIES 1775. RESIGNED 1788.
PRESIDENT OF THE UNITED STATES 1789."

1 Cent. No date (1792) **950.00**

Obv: Bust. "G. WASHINGTON PRESIDENT." Rev: Small eagle, stars above.
"UNITED STATES OF AMERICA."

Half Dollar 1792. Struck in silver . . . . ——
Half Dollar 1792. Struck in copper . . . . ——
Half Dollar 1792. Struck in silver. Similar to above but Rev. has
  larger eagle and is without stars . . . . ——

Obv: Bust. "WASHINGTON PRESIDENT." Rev: Ship. "HALFPENNY."

Half Penny 1793 . . . . **50.00**

Obv: Bust right. "GEORGE WASHINGTON." Rev: Eagle over shield.
"LIBERTY AND SECURITY 1795."

1 Penny 1795 . . . . **200.00**
Half Penny 1795 . . . . **50.00**

Obv: Bust left. "GEORGE WASHINGTON." Rev: Eagle over shield. "LIBERTY AND SECURITY."

1 Penny. No date (1795) **75.00**

Obv: Bust. "G. WASHINGTON FIRST FRIEND TO PEACE. . . ." Rev: Grate, legend around edge
and "LONDON 1795."

1 Cent 1795. The Grate Cent **40.00**

Obv: Bust. "GEORGE WASHINGTON." Rev: Circle of fifteen stars.
"SUCCESS TO THE UNITED STATES."

Success Token. No date (1795). Large size **50.00**
Success Token. As above but small size **50.00**

Obv: Bust. "GEORGIUS WASHINGTON." Rev: Crowned harp. "NORTH WALES."

Half Penny. No date (1795) **30.00**

The valuations listed in this book closely approximate how much established coin dealers will pay for any material needed in their stock.

United States Coins
(Complete from 1793 to date)

HALF CENTS

Type: Liberty head with cap facing left.

Date	Amount Minted	Value
1793	31,900	**450.00**

Type: Liberty head with cap facing right.

Date	Amount Minted	Average Circulated	Extra Fine
1794	81,600	125.00	1,250.00
1795	25,600	100.00	900.00
1796	115,500	1,750.00	10,000.00
1797	107,00	75.00	800.00

Type: Draped bust of Liberty.

Date	Amount Minted	Average Circulated	Extra Fine
1800	211,500	15.00	175.00
1802	14,400	150.00	5,000.00
1803	97,900	14.00	175.00
1804	1 million	14.00	110.00
1805	814,500	14.00	110.00
1806	356,00	14.00	110.00
1807	476,000	14.00	110.00
1808	400,000	14.00	175.00

Type: Liberty head in turban.

Date	Amount Minted	Average Circulated	Extra Fine
1809	1¼ million	9.00	40.00
1810	215,000	15.00	100.00
1811	63,100	40.00	1,250.00
1825	63,000	9.00	125.00
1826	234,000	9.00	60.00
1828	606,000	9.00	35.00
1829	487,000	9.00	35.00
1831 Proof Only	2,200	4,000	—
1832	154,000	9.00	30.00
1833	120,000	9.00	30.00
1834	141,000	9.00	30.00
1835	398,000	9.00	30.00
1836 Proof Only	—	2,750.00	—

Type: Liberty head with braided hair.

Date	Amount Minted	Average Circulated	Extra Fine
1840		1,500.00	
1841		1,500.00	
1842		1,500.00	
1843	Only proofs were	1,500.00	
1844	struck of these	1,500.00	
1845	coins.	1,500.00	
1846	The exact	1,500.00	
1847	quantities	1,500.00	
1848	minted are not	1,500.00	
1849	known.	1,500.00	
1849 large date	39,900	14.00	40.00
1850	39,800	13.00	40.00
1851	147,700	13.00	32.50
1852	Proof only	2,500.00	—
1853	129,700	13.00	32.50
1854	55,400	13.00	35.00
1855	56,500	13.00	35.00
1856	40,400	13.00	40.00
1857	32,200	27.50	50.00

LARGE CENTS

Type: Liberty head with close flowing hair; chain on Rev.

Date	Amounted Minted	Value
1793	(About 224,000 were coined of all types of 1793 cents)	**1,250.00**

Type: Liberty head with loose flowing hair; wreath on Rev.

Date	Amount Minted	Value
1793	(See above)	**425.00**

Type: Liberty head with cap.

Date	Amount Minted	Average Circulated	Extra Fine
1793	(See above)	700.00	—
1794	918,500	70.00	750.00
1795	82,000	75.00	750.00
1796	Part of 974,700	70.00	700.00

Type: Draped bust of Liberty.

Date	Amount Minted	Average Circulated	Extra Fine
1796	Part of 974,700	35.00	400.00
1797	897,500	20.00	350.00
1798	979,700	15.00	300.00
1799	904,600	450.00	—
1800	2³/₄ million	12.50	300.00
1801	1¹/₃ million	12.50	300.00
1802	3¹/₂ million	12.00	300.00
1803	2¹/₂ million	12.00	250.00
1804	756,800	250.00	3,000.00
1805	941,100	11.00	250.00
1806	348,000	13.00	350.00
1807	727,200	11.00	250.00

Type: Liberty head in turban.

Date	Amount Minted	Average Circulated	Extra Fine
1808	1 million	15.00	600.00
1809	222,900	35.00	800.00
1810	1¹/₂ million	15.00	600.00
1811	218,000	25.00	700.00
1812	1 million	13.00	600.00
1813	418,000	16.00	700.00
1814	357,800	13.00	650.00

Type: Liberty head in coronet.

Date	Amount Minted	Average Circulated	Extra Fine
1816	2³/₄ million	4.50	60.00
1817	4 million	4.50	60.00
1818	3¹/₄ million	4.00	60.00

1819	2²/₃ million	4.50	60.00
1820	4¹/₂ million	4.50	60.00
1821	389,000	9.00	175.00
1822	2 million	4.00	60.00
1823	855,700	4.00	60.00
1824	1¹/₂ million	4.00	60.00
1825	1¹/₂ million	4.00	60.00
1826	1¹/₂ million	4.00	60.00
1827	2¹/₃ million	4.00	60.00
1828	2¹/₄ million	4.00	60.00
1829	1¹/₂ million	4.00	60.00
1830	1³/₄ million	4.00	60.00
1831	3¹/₃ million	4.00	50.00
1832	2¹/₃ million	4.00	50.00
1833	2³/₄ million	4.00	50.00
1834	2 million	4.00	50.00
1835	Part of 4 million	4.00	50.00
1836	2 million	4.00	50.00
1837	5¹/₂ million	4.00	40.00
1838	6¹/₃ million	4.00	40.00
1839	3¹/₄ million	4.00	50.00

Type: Liberty head with braided hair

Date	Amount Minted	Average Circulated	Extra Fine
1840	2¹/₂ million	3.50	25.00
1841	1¹/₂ million	3.50	25.00
1842	2¹/₃ million	3.50	25.00
1843	2¹/₂ million	3.50	25.00
1844	2¹/₂ million	3.50	25.00
1845	4 million	3.50	30.00
1846	4 million	3.50	25.00
1847	6¹/₄ million	3.50	25.00
1848	6¹/₂ million	3.50	25.00
1849	4¹/₄ million	3.50	25.00
1850	4¹/₂ million	3.50	25.00
1851	10 million	3.50	25.00
1852	5 million	3.50	25.00
1853	6²/₃ million	3.50	25.00
1854	4¹/₄ million	3.50	30.00
1855	1¹/₂ million	3.50	25.00
1856	2²/₃ million	3.50	25.00
1857	333,500	12.00	45.00

SMALL CENTS

Type: Flying eagle—Copper-Nickel

Date	Amount Minted	Value	Date	Amount Minted	Value
1856	About 1000	**2,000.00**	1858	24²/₃ million	**6.00**
1857	17¹/₂ million	**5.00**			

Type: Indian head; without shield on Rev.—Copper-Nickel

Date	Amount Minted	Value
1859	36¹/₃ million	**4.00**

Type: Indian head; with shield on Rev.—Copper-Nickel

Date	Amount Minted	Value	Date	Amount Minted	Value
1860	20½ million	**2.50**	1863	49¾ million	**1.50**
1861	10 million	**8.00**	1864	13¾ million	**7.50**
1862	28 million	**1.75**			

(The bronze Indian Head Cents which follow are of the same design as the Copper-Nickel Cents above)

Type: Indian head—Bronze

(The "S" mint mark of 1908 and 1909 is on the Rev., under the wreath)

Date	Amount Minted	Value	Date	Amount Minted	Value
1864	39¼ million	**3.00**	1888	37½ million	**.70**
1864-L	Part of above	**20.00**	1889	48¾ million	**.70**
1865	35½ million	**2.50**	1890	57¼ million	**.70**
1866	9¾ million	**12.00**	1891	47 million	**.70**
1867	9¾ million	**12.00**	1892	37⅔ million	**.70**
1868	10¼ million	**12.00**	1893	46⅔ million	**.70**
1869	6½ million	**20.00**	1894	16¾ million	**.80**
1870	5¼ million	**15.00**	1895	38⅓ million	**.40**
1871	4 million	**16.00**	1896	39 million	**.40**
1872	4 million	**27.50**	1897	50½ million	**.40**
1873	11⅔ million	**5.00**	1898	49¾ million	**.40**
1874	14¼ million	**5.00**	1899	53⅔ million	**.40**
1875	13½ million	**5.00**	1900	66¾ million	**.40**
1876	8 million	**11.00**	1901	79⅔ million	**.40**
1877	852,500	**150.00**	1902	87½ million	**.40**
1878	5¾ million	**11.00**	1903	85 million	**.40**
1879	16¼ million	**2.25**	1904	61½ million	**.40**
1880	39 million	**1.00**	1905	80¾ million	**.40**
1881	39¼ million	**1.00**	1906	96 million	**.40**
1882	38½ million	**1.00**	1907	108¼ million	**.40**
1883	45½ million	**.75**	1908	32½ million	**.40**
1884	23¼ million	**1.00**	1908-S	1 million	**15.00**
1885	11¾ million	**1.75**	1909	14½ million	**.50**
1886	17⅔ million	**1.50**	1909-S	309,000	**110.00**
1887	45½ million	**.70**			

Type: Lincoln head
(The mint mark is on the Obv., under the date)

Date	Amount Minted	Value	Date	Amount Minted	Value
1909-VDB	28 million	.75	1926-D	28 million	.05
1909-S-VDB	484,000	200.00	1926-S	4⅔ million	1.50
1909	72¾ million	.15	1927	144½ million	.03
1909-S	1¾ million	15.00	1927-D	27¼ million	.05
1910	146¾ million	.05	1927-S	14½ million	.15
1910-S	6 million	3.50	1928	134 million	.02
1911	101¼ million	.05	1928-D	31¼ million	.03
1911-D	12¾ million	2.00	1928-S	17⅓ million	.05
1911-S	4 million	8.00	1929	185½ million	.02
1912	68¼ million	.05	1929-D	41¾ million	.03
1912-D	10½ million	1.75	1929-S	50 million	.05
1912-S	4½ million	5.00	1930	157½ million	.02
1913	76½ million	.05	1930-D	40 million	.03
1913-D	15¾ million	1.00	1930-S	24½ million	.03
1913-S	6 million	2.50	1931	19½ million	.10
1914	75¼ million	.05	1931-D	4½ million	1.25
1914-D	1¼ million	40.00	1931-S	866,000	20.00
1914-S	4 million	4.00	1932	9 million	.75
1915	29 million	.35	1932-D	10½ million	.40
1915-D	22 million	.15	1933	14½ million	.40
1915-S	4¾ million	2.75	1933-D	6¼ million	.65
1916	131¾ million	.05	1934	219 million	.02
1916-D	36 million	.10	1934-D	28½ million	.03
1916-S	22½ million	.25	1935	245½ million	.02
1917	196½ million	.05	1935-D	47 million	.03
1917-D	55 million	.10	1935-S	38¾ million	.04
1917-S	32⅔ million	.15	1936	309¾ million	.02
1918	288 million	.05	1936-D	40⅔ million	.03
1918-D	47¾ million	.10	1936-S	29 million	.04
1918-S	34¾ million	.15	1937	309¼ million	.02
1919	392 million	.05	1937-D	50½ million	.03
1919-D	57¼ million	.10	1937-S	34½ million	.04
1919-S	139¾ million	.05	1938	156¾ million	.02
1920	310¼ million	.03	1938-D	20 million	.05
1920-D	49½ million	.05	1938-S	15¼ million	.10
1920-S	46¼ million	.05	1939	316½ million	.02
1921	39¼ million	.05	1939-D	15¼ million	.10
1921-S	15½ million	.25	1939-S	52 million	.05
1922-D	7¼ million	1.75	1940	586¾ million	.02
1922	Plain Part of above	70.00	1940-D	81 ½ million	.03
1923	74¾ million	.03	1940-S	113 million	.04
1923-S	8¾ million	.50	1941	887 million	.02
1924	75¼ million	.03	1941-D	128¾ million	.03
1924-D	2½ million	3.50	1941-S	92½ million	.03
1924-S	11¾ million	.25	1942	657¾ million	.02
1925	140 million	.03	1942-D	206¾ million	.03
1925-D	22⅔ million	.10	1942-S	85¾ million	.04
1925-S	26½ million	.05	1943	684⅔ million	.03
1926	157 million	.03	1943-D	217¾ million	.05

Date	Amount Minted	Value	Date	Amount Minted	Value
1943-S	191²/₃ million	.07	1951	294²/₃ million	.02
1944	1¹/₂ billion	.02	1951-D	625¹/₂ million	.02
1944-D	430²/₃ million	.02	1951-S	101 million	.02
1944-S	232³/₄ million	.03	1952	187 million	.02
1945	1 billion	.02	1952-D	746 million	.02
1945-D	226¹/₃ million	.02	1952-S	137³/₄ million	.02
1945-S	181³/₄ million	.03	1953	257 million	.02
1946	991³/₄ million	.02	1953-D	700¹/₂ million	.02
1946-D	315³/₄ million	.02	1953-S	182 million	.02
1946-S	198 million	.03	1954	72 million	.02
1947	190¹/₂ million	.02	1954-D	251¹/₂ million	.02
1947-D	194³/₄ million	.02	1954-S	96¹/₄ million	.02
1947-S	99 million	.03	1955	331 million	.02
1948	317²/₃ million	.02	1955	double die. (Very Fine)	200.00
1948-D	172²/₃ million	.02	1955-D	563¹/₂ million	.02
1948-S	81³/₄ million	.03	1955-S	44²/₃ million	.03
1949	217¹/₂ million	.02	1956	421 million	.02
1949-D	154¹/₃ million	.02	1956-D	1 billion	.02
1949-S	64¹/₃ million	.03	1957	282¹/₂ million	.02
1950	272³/₄ million	.02	1957-D	1 billion	.02
1950-D	335 million	.02	1958	252¹/₂ million	.02
1950-S	118¹/₂ million	.03	1958-D	801 million	.02

*(The valuations in this book are based on the coins
being in G-VG condition, unless otherwise noted.)*

Type: Lincoln head with the Lincoln Memorial on the reverse

Date	Amount Minted	Value	Date	Amount Minted	Value
1959	609³/₄ million	.01	1969-D	4 billion	.01
1959-D	1¹/₄ billion	.01	1969-S	544¹/₃ million	.01
1960	586¹/₂ million	.01	1970	1³/₄ billion	.01
1960	Small Date (unc)	.50	1970-D	2³/₄ billion	.01
1960-D	1¹/₂ billion	.01	1970-S	690¹/₂ million	.01
1960-D	Small Date	.02	1970-S	Small Date (unc)	15.00
1961	753¹/₃ million	.01	1971	2 billion	.01
1961-D	1³/₄ billion	.01	1971-D	3 billion	.01
1962	606 million	.01	1971-S	525 million	.01
1962-D	1³/₄ billion	.01	1972	3 billion	.01
1963	754 million	.01	1972	double die. (unc.)	75.00
1963-D	1³/₄ billion	.01	1972-D	2²/₃ billion	.01
1964	2²/₃ billion	.01	1972-S	380 million	.01
1964-D	3³/₄ billion	.01	1973	3³/₄ billion	.01
1965	1¹/₂ billion	.01	1973-D	3¹/₂ billion	.01
1966	2¹/₄ billion	.01	1973-S	320 million	.01
1967	3 billion	.01	1974	4¹/₄ billion	.01
1968	1³/₄ billion	.01	1974-D	4¹/₄ billion	.01
1968-D	2³/₄ billion	.01	1974-S	412 million	.01
1968-S	258¹/₄ million	.01	1975	5¹/₂ billion	.01
1969	1.2 billion	(unc.) .10	1975-D	4¹/₂ billion	.01

Date	Amount Minted	Value	Date	Amount Minted	Value
1975-S	proof only 3 million	1.50	1984-D	5.5 billion	.01
1976	4½ billion	.01	1984-S	proof only 3 million	4.50
1976-D	4¼ billion	.01	1985	5.5 billion	.01
1976-S	proof only 4 million	.85	1985-D	5.25 billion	.01
1977	4½ billion	.01	1985-S	proof only 3.4 million	1.00
1977-D	4¼ billion	.01	1986	4.5 billion	.01
1977-S	proof only 3¼ million	.60	1986-D	4.4 billion	.01
1978	5½ billion	.01	1986-S	proof only 3 million	3.50
1978-D	4¼ billion	.01	1987	4.7 billion	.01
1978-S	proof only 3 million	.60	1987-D	4.9 billion	.01
1979	6 billion	.01	1987-S	proof only 3¾ million	1.50
1979-D	4¼ billion	.01	1988	6.1 billion	.01
1979-S	proof only 3¾ million	.60	1988-D	5¼ billion	.01
1980	7½ billion	.01	1988-S	proof only 3.23 million	1.50
1980-D	5 billion	.01	1989	7.26 billion	.01
1980-S	proof only 3½ million	.50	1989-D	5.34 billion	.01
1981	7½ billion	.01	1989-S	proof only	2.00
1981-D	5½ billion	.01	1990		.01
1981-S	proof only 4 million	.30	1990-D		.01
1982	copper, lg. date	.02	1990-S	proof only	2.25
1982	copper, sm. date	.02	1991	5.16 billion	.01
1982	zinc, lg. date	.01	1991-D	4.16 billion	.01
1982	zinc, sm. date	.01	1991-S	proof only	3.75
	(9 billion, all types)		1992		.01
1982-D	copper, lg. date	.01	1992-D		.01
1982-D	zinc, lg. date	.05	1992-S	proof only	2.50
1982-D	zinc, sm. date	.01	1993		.01
	(6 billion, all types)	**1993-D**	1993-D		.01
1982-S	3.8 million proofs	.85	1993-S	proof only	2.00
1983	7½ billion	.01	1994		.01
1983	double die (rev.) (unc.)	60.00	1994-D		.01
1983-D	6½ billion	.01	1994-S	proof only	2.00
1983-S	proof only 3¼ million	1.25			
1984	8.1 billion	.01			
1984	double die (rev.) (unc.)	35.00			

2 CENT PIECES

Type: Bronze with shield on Obv. and the value on the Rev.

Date	Amount Minted	Average Circulated	Extra Fine
1864 Large motto	19¾ million	2.75	15.00
1864 Small motto	Part of above	25.00	125.00
1865	13⅔ million	2.50	15.00
1866	3¼ million	2.50	15.00
1867	3 million	2.50	15.00
1868	3 million	2.50	15.00
1869	1½ million	3.50	17.50
1870	861,250	2.75	16.00
1871	721,250	4.00	25.00
1872	65,000	35.00	200.00
1873	600 proofs	700.00	—

3 CENT PIECES—SILVER

Plain star and plain III
1851–1853

Star with borders; sprig and arrows of the III
1854–1873

Type: Large star, the Rev. has the Roman Numeral III for the value.

(The "O" mint mark is on the Rev., to the right of the III)

Date	Amount Minted	Average Circulated	Extra Fine
1851	5½ million	5.00	25.00
1851-O	720,000	7.60	50.00
1852	18⅔ million	5.00	20.00
1853	11½ million	5.00	20.00
1854	671,000	5.00	40.00
1855	139,000	7.00	65.00
1856	1½ million	5.00	30.00
1857	1 million	5.00	30.00
1858	1⅔ million	5.00	30.00
1859	365,000	5.50	20.00
1860	287,000	6.50	25.00
1861	498,000	5.50	30.00
1862	363,550	6.50	35.00

1863	21,500 proofs	200.00	—
1864	470 proofs	300.00	—
1865	8,500 proofs	300.00	—
1866	22,700 proofs	200.00	—
1867	4,625 proofs	200.00	—
1868	4,100 proofs	200.00	—
1869	5,100 proofs	250.00	—
1870	4,000 proofs	200.00	—
1871	4,260 proofs	200.00	—
1872	1,950 proofs	300.00	—
1873	600 proofs	400.00	—

3 CENT PIECES—NICKEL

Type: Liberty head. The Rev. has the Roman numeral III for the value.

Date	Amount Minted	Average Circulated	Extra Fine
1865	11½ million	3.00	7.00
1866	4¾ million	3.00	7.00
1867	4 million	3.00	7.00
1868	3¼ million	3.00	7.00
1869	1⅔ million	3.00	7.50
1870	1½ million	3.00	7.50
1871	604,000	3.00	7.50
1872	862,000	3.00	7.50
1873	1¼ million	3.00	7.50
1874	790,000	3.00	7.50
1875	228,000	3.25	10.00
1876	162,000	4.00	14.00
1877	510 proofs	500.00	—
1878	2,350 proofs	250.00	—
1879	41,200	21.00	35.00
1880	25,000	25.00	60.00
1881	1⅛ million	3.00	7.00
1882	25,300	25.00	50.00
1883	10,600	55.00	100.00
1884	5,650	125.00	200.00
1885	4,800	175.00	350.00
1886	4,300 proofs	200.00	—
1887	7,960	100.00	225.00
1888	41,000	15.00	32.50
1889	21,600	30.00	55.00

NICKELS

With rays on Rev. 1866–1867   *Without rays on Rev. 1867–1883*

Type: Shield. The U.S. shield is on the obv. and the value is on the Rev.

Date	Amount Minted	Value	Date	Amount Minted	Value
1866	14³/₄ million	5.00	1875	2 million	5.50
1867 With rays	31 million	6.50	1876	2¹/₂ million	4.00
1867 No rays	Part of above	3.50	1877	510 proofs	500.00
1868	28³/₄ million	3.50	1878	2,350 proofs	250.00
1869	16¹/₂ million	3.50	1879	29,100	125.00
1870	4³/₄ million	4.00	1880	19,950	135.00
1871	561,000	13.00	1881	72,400	75.00
1872	6 million	4.00	1882	11¹/₂ million	4.00
1873	4¹/₂ million	4.00	1883	1¹/₂ million	4.00
1874	3¹/₂ million	4.50			

Without "Cents" on Rev. 1883   *With "Cents" on Rev. 1883*

Type: Liberty head.

(The mint marks of 1912 are on the Rev., to the left of "Cents" and under the dot)

Date	Amount Minted	Value	Date	Amount Minted	Value
1883 Without "Cents"	5¹/₂ million	1.00	1901	26¹/₂ million	.25
1883 With "Cents"	16 million	3.00	1902	31¹/₂ million	.25
1884	11¹/₄ million	3.50	1903	28 million	.25
1885	1¹/₂ million	90.00	1904	21¹/₂ million	.25
1886	3¹/₃ million	20.00	1905	29³/₄ million	.25
1887	15¹/₄ million	2.00	1906	38²/₃ million	.25
1888	10³/₄ million	3.25	1907	39¹/₄ million	.25
1889	15³/₄ million	1.50	1908	22²/₃ million	.25
1890	16¹/₄ million	2.00	1909	11¹/₂ million	.25
1891	16³/₄ million	1.50	1910	30¹/₄ million	.20
1892	11¹/₂ million	1.50	1911	39¹/₂ million	.20
1893	13¹/₃ million	1.50	1912	26¹/₄ million	.20
1894	5¹/₂ million	2.50	1912-D	8¹/₂ million	.30
1895	10 million	1.00	1912-S	238,000	17.50
1896	8³/₄ million	1.00	1913	5 pieces struck. All	
1897	20¹/₂ million	.50		are accounted for in	
1898	12¹/₂ million	.50		collections and it is	
1899	26 million	.30		not possible to find	
1900	27¹/₄ million	.25		one.	

Type I. Buffalo on hilly mound
1913

Type II. Buffalo on more level mound
1913–1938

Type: Buffalo and Indian head.

(The mint marks are on the Rev., under "Five Cents")

Date	Amount Minted	Value	Date	Amount Minted	Value
1913-I	31 million	2.00	1916-D	13¹/₃ million	2.25
1913-D-I	5¹/₃ million	3.00	1916-S	11³/₄ million	1.50
1913-S-I	2 million	5.00	1917	51¹/₂ million	.50
1913-II	29³/₄ million	1.50	1917-D	10 million	2.25
1913-D-II	4¹/₄ million	15.00	1917-S	4¹/₄ million	1.75
1913-S-II	1¹/₄ million	40.00	1918	32 million	.50
1914	20²/₃ million	2.00	1918-D	8¹/₃ million	2.00
1914-D	4 million	12.50	1918/17D		200.00
1914-S	3¹/₂ million	2.00	1918-S	4³/₄ million	1.50
1915	21 million	1.00	1919	60³/₄ million	.40
1915-D	7¹/₂ million	2.50	1919-D	8 million	2.00
1915-S	7¹/₂ million	4.00	1919-S	7¹/₂ million	1.50
1916	63¹/₂ million	.50	1920	63 million	.30
1916, over 16		700.00	1920-D	9¹/₂ million	2.60
1920-S	²/₃ million	.80	1929	36¹/₂ million	.10
1921	10²/₃ million	.50	1929-D	8¹/₃ million	.40
1921-S	1¹/₂ million	8.00	1929-S	7³/₄ million	.20
1923	35³/₄ million	.25	1930	22³/₄ million	.10
1923-S	6¹/₄ million	1.00	1930-S	5¹/₂ million	.15
1924	21²/₃ million	.20	1931-S	1¹/₄ million	1.25
1924-D	5¹/₄ million	1.25	1934	20¹/₄ million	.10
1924-S	1¹/₂ million	2.50	1934-D	7¹/₂ million	.10
1925	35¹/₂ million	.25	1935	58¹/₄ million	.10
1925-D	4¹/₂ million	1.75	1935-D	12 million	.10
1925-S	6¹/₄ million	.75	1935-S	10¹/₂ million	.10
1926	44²/₃ million	.15	1936	119 million	.10
1926-D	5²/₃ million	1.00	1936-D	24¹/₂ million	.10
1926-S	970,000	3.00	1936-S	15 million	.10
1927	38 million	.15	1937	79¹/₂ million	.10
1927-D	5³/₄ million	.50	1937-D	17³/₄ million	.10
1927-S	3¹/₂ million	.25	1937-D 3-legged buffalo		65.00
1928	23¹/₂ million	.15	1937-S	5²/₃ million	.10
1928-D	6¹/₂ million	.40	1938-D	7 million	.10
1928-S	7 million	.25	1938-D/D		.50
			1938-D/S		1.50

Normal type
1938–1942 & 1946 to date

Silver content type with large
Mint Mark on Rev.
1942–1945

Type: Jefferson head.

(From 1938–1942 and 1946–1964, the mint marks are on the Rev. to the right of the building. On the silver content nickels, 1942–1945, the mint marks are much larger and are over the building. From 1968 to date, the mint marks are on the obverse under the date.)

Date	Amount Minted	Value	Date	Amount Minted	Value
1938	19½ million	.10	1940-D	43½ million	.06
1938-D	5½ million	.20	1940-S	39⅔ million	.06
1938-S	4 million	.50	1941	203¼ million	.06
1939	120⅔ million	.06	1941-D	53½ million	.06
1939-D	3½ million	1.00	1941-S	43½ million	.06
1939-S	6⅔ million	.15	1942	49¾ million	.06
1940	176½ million	.06	1942-D	14 million	.10

Silver content Nickels with large mint mark on reverse.

Date	Amount Minted	Value	Date	Amount Minted	Value
1942-P	56 million	.12	1944-D	32½ million	.12
1942-S	33 million	.12	1944-S	21⅔ million	.12
1943-P	27¼ million	.12	1945-P	119½ million	.12
1943-D	15¼ million	.15	1945-D	37¼ million	.12
1943-S	104 million	.12	1945-S	59 million	.12
1944-P	119¼ million	.12			

Standard composition Nickels

(Prices are for uncirculated coins)

Date	Amount Minted	Value	Date	Amount Minted	Value
1946	161 million	.10	1954-D	117¼ million	.07
1946-D	45¼ million	.25	1954-S	29½ million	.07
1946-S	13½ million	.20	1955	8¼ million	.15
1947	95 million	.10	1955-D	74½ million	.06
1947-D	37¾ million	.25	1956	35⅓ million	.05
1947-S	24¾ million	.20	1956-D	67¼ million	.05
1948	89½ million	.10	1957	38½ million	.05
1948-D	44¾ million	.30	1957-D	136¾ million	.05
1948-S	11½ million	.30	1958	17 million	.05
1949	60⅔ million	.20	1958-D	141¾ million	.05
1949-D	35¼ million	.30	1959	27¼ million	.05
1949-S	9¾ million	.50	1959-D	160¾ million	.05
1950	9¾ million	.50	1960	55½ million	.05
1950-D	2⅔ million	2.50	1960-D	192½ million	.05
1951	28⅔ million	.25	1961	73⅔ million	.05
1951-D	20½ million	.40	1961-D	229¼ million	.05
1951-S	7¾ million	.50	1962	97⅓ million	.05
1952	64 million	.15	1962-D	280¼ million	.05
1952-D	30⅔ million	.20	1963	175¾ million	.05
1952-S	20112 million	.25	1963-D	276¾ million	.05
1953	46¾ million	.07	1964	1 billion	.05
1953-D	59¾ million	.07	1964-D	1¾ billion	.05
1953-S	19¼ million	.08	1965	136 million	.05
1954	48 million	.07	1966	156¼ million	.05

Date	Amount Minted	Value	Date	Amount Minted	Value
1967	107½ million	.05	1983	561½ million	.05
1968-D	91¼ million	.05	1983-D	536¾ million	.05
1968-S	100⅓ million	.05	1983-S	3¼ million proofs	.75
1969-D	202¾ million	.05	1984	746 million	.05
1969-S	120¼ million	.05	1984-D	500 million	.05
1970-D	515½ million	.05	1984-S	3.06 million	1.00
1970-S	238¾ million	.05	1985	647 million	.05
1971	106.8 million	.05	1985-D	460 million	.05
1971-D	316 million	.05	1985-S	3.3 million proofs	.50
1971-S	3¼ million proofs	.35	1986	537 million	.05
1972	202 million	.05	1986-D	362 million	.05
1972-D	351⅔ million	.05	1986-S	3 million proofs	2.00
1972-S	3¼ million proofs	.35	1987	371 million	.05
1973	384½ million	.05	1987-D	411 million	.05
1973-D	261½ million	.05	1987-S	3¾ million proofs	.50
1973-S	2¾ million proofs	.35	1988	771½ million	.05
1974	601¾ million	.05	1988-D	663¾ million	.05
1974-D	277½ million	.05	1988-S	3.23 million proofs	1.00
1974-S	2⅔ million proofs	.50	1989	898.8 million	.05
1975	181¾ million	.05	1989-D	570.8 million	.05
1975-D	402 million	.05	1989-S	3.2 million proofs	.75
1975-S	2¾ million proofs	.30	1990	6661.6 million	.05
1976	367 million	.05	1990-D	664 million	.05
1976-D	564 million	.05	1990-S	3.3 million proofs	.75
1976-S	4¼ million proofs	.30	1991	614.1 million	.05
1977	585½ million	.05	1991-D	436.5 million	.05
1977-D	297½ million	.05	1991-S	287 million proofs	.75
1977-S	3¼ million proofs	.25	1992	399.5 million	.05
1978	391½ million	.05	1992-D	450.5 million	.05
1978-D	313 million	.05	1992-S	4.1 million proofs	1.00
1978-S	3¼ million proofs	.25	1993	412.1 million	.05
1979	463¼ million	.05	1993-D	406.1 million	.05
1979-D	325¾ million	.05	1993-S	3.4 million proofs	.75
1979-S	3⅔ million proofs	.25	1994		.05
1980	600 million	.05	1994-D		.05
1980-D	502⅓ million	.05	1994-S	proofs	.75
1980-S	3½ million proofs	.25			
1981	657½ million	.05			
1981-D	364¾ million	.05			
1981-S	4 million proofs	.40			
1982	292⅓ million	.05			
1982-D	373¾ million	.05			
1982-S	3.8 million proofs	.40			

HALF DIMES

Type: Liberty head with flowing hair.

Date	Amount Minted	Value
1794		400.00
1795		300.00

(The combined coinage of 1794 and 1795 was 86,416 pieces. The exact amount of each year is not known.)

Type: Draped bust of Liberty; small eagle on Rev.

Date	Amount Minted	Value
1796	10,200	450.00
1797	44,500	400.00

Type: Draped bust of Liberty; large eagle on Rev.

Date	Amount Minted	Value
1800	24,000	275.00
1801	33,900	300.00
1802	13,000	5,000.00
1803	37,800	250.00
1805	15,600	350.00

Type: Bust of Liberty wearing cap.

Date	Amount Minted	Value
1829	1¼ million	4.00
1830	1¼ million	4.00
1831	1¼ million	4.00
1832	965,000	4.00
1833	1½ million	4.00
1834	1½ million	4.00
1835	2¾ million	4.00
1836	2 million	4.00
1837	2¼ million	4.00

Type: Liberty seated; no stars on Obv.

(The mint mark is under the value on the Rev.)

Date	Amount Minted	Value
1837	2¼ million	12.00
1838-O	70,000	30.00

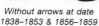

Without arrows at date
1838–1853 & 1856–1859

With arrows at date
1853–1855

Type: Liberty seated; with stars on Obv.

(The mint mark is under the value on the Rev.)

Date	Amount Minted	Value	Date	Amount Minted	Value
1838	2¼ million	3.00	1842	815,000	2.00
1839	1 million	3.25	1842-O	350,000	11.00
1839-O	1 million	4.00	1843	1¼ million	2.00
1840	1⅓ million	2.00	1844	430,000	3.00
1840-O	935,000	4.00	1844-O	220,000	27.00
1840-w/drapery		5.00	1845	1½ million	2.00
1840-D w/drapery		6.00	1846	27,000	70.00
1841	1¼ million	2.50	1847	1¼ million	2.00
1841-O	815,000	3.00	1848	668,000	3.00

Date	Amount Minted	Value	Date	Amount Minted	Value
1848-O	600,000	3.00	1854-O	1½ million	2.50
1849	1⅓ million	2.00	1855	1¾ million	2.00
1849-O	140,000	10.00	1855-O	600,000	3.50
1850	955,000	2.00	1856	4¾ million	2.00
1850-O	690,000	3.00	1856-O	1 million	3.00
1851	781,000	2.75	1857	7¼ million	2.00
1851-O	860,000	4.50	1857-O	1⅓ million	3.00
1852	1 million	2.00	1858	3½ million	2.00
1852-O	260,000	10.00	1858-O	1⅔ million	2.50
1853 No Arr.	*	8.00	1859	340,000	4.00
1853-O No Arr.	*	35.00	1859-O	560,000	3.00
1853 Arr.	13½ million	2.00			
1853-O Arr.	2⅓ million	2.00	*The figures for the No Arrow coinage are		
1854	5¾ million	2.00	included in the figures for the Arrow coinage.		

Type: Liberty seated; with "United States of America" on Obv.

(The mint marks are on the Rev., under or within the wreath)

Date	Amount Minted	Value	Date	Amount Minted	Value
1860	799,000	2.00	1867-S	120,000	5.00
1860-O	1 million	3.00	1868	85,900	10.00
1861	3¼ million	2.00	1868-S	280,000	3.00
1862	1½ million	2.00	1869	208,600	2.50
1863	18,500	45.00	1869-S	230,000	3.00
1863-S	100,000	6.50	1870	536,600	2.00
1864	48,470	100.00	1871	1½ million	2.00
1864-S	90,000	7.50	1871-S	161,000	6.00
1865	13,500	80.00	1872	3 million	2.00
1865-S	120,000	5.00	1872-S	837,000	2.00
1866	10,700	80.00	1873	712,600	2.50
1866-S	120,000	6.00	1873-S	324,000	3.00
1867	8,600	150.00			

DIMES

Type: Draped bust of Liberty; small eagle on Rev.

Date	Amount Minted	Value	Date	Amount Minted	Value
1796	22,100	400.00	1797	25,300	450.00

Type: Draped bust of Liberty; large eagle on Rev.

Date	Amount Minted	Value	Date	Amount Minted	Value
1798	27,500	250.00	1803	33,000	250.00
1800	21,800	250.00	1804	8,300	400.00
1801	34,600	250.00	1805	120,800	200.00
1802	11,000	350.00	1807	165,000	200.00

Large Size 1809–1828   Reduced Size 1828–1837

Type: Bust of Liberty wearing cap.

Date	Amount Minted	Value	Date	Amount Minted	Value
1809	44,700	75.00	1828	125,000	7.00
1811	65,200	17.50	1829	770,000	6.00
1814	421,500	6.00	1830	510,000	4.00
1820	942,600	6.00	1831	771,300	4.00
1821	1¼ million	6.00	1832	522,500	4.00
1822	100,000	150.00	1833	485,000	4.00
1823	440,000	5.00	1834	635,000	4.00
1824	Unknown	10.00	1835	1⅓ million	4.00
1825	510,000	6.00	1836	1¼ million	4.00
1827	1¼ million	6.00	1837	1 million	5.00

Type: Liberty seated; no stars on Obv.

(The mint mark is under the value on the Rev.)

Date	Amount Minted	Value	Date	Amount Minted	Value
1837	Unknown	12.00	1838-O	402,400	15.00

Without arrows at date
1838–1853 & 1856–1860

With arrows at date
1853–1855

Type: Liberty seated; with stars on Obv.

(The mint marks is under the value on the Rev.)

Date	Amount Minted	Value	Date	Amount Minted	Value
1838	2 million	3.00	1851-O	400,000	3.00
1839	1 million	2.50	1852	1½ million	1.50
1839-O	1¼ million	2.75	1852-O	430,000	3.25
1840	1½ million	2.00	1853 No Arr.	12¼ million	14.00
1840-O	1¼ million	2.75	1853 Arr.		1.50
1841	1⅔ million	1.50	1853-O	1 million	2.00
1841-O	2 million	1.50	1854	4½ million	1.50
1842	2 million	1.50	1854-O	1¾ million	1.75
1842-O	2 million	2.00	1855	2 million	1.50
1843	1⅓ million	1.50	1856	5¾ million	1.50
1843-O	150,000	15.00	1856-O	1¼ million	1.50
1844	72,500	30.00	1856-S	70,000	30.00
1845	1¾ million	1.50	1857	5½ million	1.50
1845-O	230,000	7.00	1857-O	1½ million	1.50
1846	31,300	28.00	1858	1½ million	1.50
1847	245,000	4.50	1858-O	290,000	3.25
1848	451,500	3.75	1858-S	60,000	25.00
1849	839,000	1.75	1859	430,000	1.50
1849-O	300,000	3.75	1859-O	480,000	2.00
1850	2 million	1.50	1859-S	60,000	30.00
1850-O	510,000	2.00	1860-S	140,000	6.00
1851	1 million	1.50			

Without arrows at date
1860–1873 & 1875–1891

With arrows at date
1873–1874

Type: Liberty seated; with "United States of America" on Obv.

(The mint marks are on the Rev., under or within the wreath)

Date	Amount Minted	Value	Date	Amount Minted	Value
1860	607,000	2.00	1872	2½ million	1.50
1860-O	40,000	125.00	1872-S	190,000	7.00
1861	2 million	1.50	1872-CC	24,000	150.00
1861-S	172,500	8.50	1873 No Arr.	1¾ million	1.50
1862	847,500	2.00	1873 Arr.	2¼ million	3.00
1862-S	180,700	8.50	1873-S	455,000	3.00
1863	14,500	75.00	1873-CC	18,800	250.00
1863-S	157,500	8.50	1874	3 million	3.00
1864	39,000	85.00	1874-S	240,000	8.00
1864-S	230,000	6.00	1874-CC	10,800	500.00
1865	10,500	50.00	1875	10½ million	1.50
1865-S	175,000	6.00	1875-S	9 million	1.50
1866	8,700	100.00	1875-CC	4⅔ million	1.50
1866-S	135,000	6.00	1876	11½ million	1.50
1867	6,600	125.00	1876-S	10½ million	1.50
1867-S	140,000	6.00	1876-CC	8¼ million	1.50
1868	466,200	2.00	1877	7½ million	1.50
1868-S	260,000	4.00	1877-S	2½ million	1.50
1869	256,600	3.00	1877-CC	7¾ million	1.50
1869-S	450,000	2.50	1878	1⅔ million	1.50
1870	471,500	2.00	1878-CC	200,000	12.50
1870-S	50,000	80.00	1879	15,100	60.00
1871	753,600	2.00	1880	37,400	35.00
1871-S	320,000	6.00	1881	25,000	40.00
1871-CC	20,100	275.00	1882	4 million	1.50

Date	Amount Minted	Value	Date	Amount Minted	Value
1883	7²/₃ million	**1.50**	1888	5¹/₂ million	**1.50**
1884	3¹/₃ million	**1.50**	1888-S	1³/₄ million	**1.50**
1884-S	565,000	**5.50**	1889	7¹/₃ million	**1.50**
1885	2¹/₂ million	**1.50**	1889-S	972,700	**3.50**
1885-S	43,700	**125.00**	1890	10 million	**1.50**
1886	6¹/₂ million	**1.50**	1890-S	1¹/₂ million	**1.50**
1886-S	206,500	**20.00**	1891	15¹/₃ million	**1.50**
1887	11¹/₄ million	**1.50**	1891-O	4¹/₂ million	**1.50**
1887-S	4¹/₂ million	**1.50**	1891-S	3¹/₄ million	**1.50**

Type: Liberty head.

(The mint marks are on the Rev., under the wreath)

Date	Amount Minted	Value	Date	Amount Minted	Value
1892	12 million	**1.00**	1905	14¹/₂ million	**.40**
1892-O	3³/₄ million	**2.00**	1905-O	3¹/₂ million	**.85**
1892-S	990,700	**12.50**	1905-S	6³/₄ million	**.85**
1893	3¹/₂ million	**2.50**	1906	20 million	**.40**
1893-O	1³/₄ million	**5.00**	1906-D	4 million	**.75**
1893-S	2¹/₂ million	**2.50**	1906-O	2²/₃ million	**1.00**
1894	1¹/₂ million	**2.75**	1906-S	3¹/₄ million	**.60**
1894-O	720,000	**10.00**	1907	22³/₄ million	**.40**
1894-S	24	**Rare**	1907-D	4 million	**.50**
1895	690,900	**25.00**	1907-O	5 million	**.50**
1895-O	440,000	**60.00**	1907-S	3¹/₄ million	**.75**
1895-S	1 million	**8.00**	1908	10²/₃ million	**.35**
1896	2 million	**2.00**	1908-D	7¹/₂ million	**.35**
1896-O	610,000	**17.50**	1908-O	1³/₄ million	**.75**
1896-S	575,000	**15.00**	1908-S	3¹/₄ million	**.60**
1897	10³/₄ million	**.40**	1909	10¹/₄ million	**.40**
1897-O	666,000	**15.00**	1909-D	954,000	**1.25**
1897-S	1¹/₃ million	**3.00**	1909-O	2¹/₄ million	**.65**
1898	16¹/₃ million	**.40**	1909-S	1 million	**1.25**
1898-O	2¹/₄ million	**3.00**	1910	1¹/₂ million	**.40**
1898-S	1³/₄ million	**1.50**	1910-D	3¹/₂ million	**.40**
1899	19¹/₂ million	**.40**	1910-S	1¹/₄ million	**.50**
1899-O	2²/₃ million	**2.50**	1911	19 million	**.35**
1899-S	1³/₄ million	**1.50**	1911-D	11¹/₄ million	**.35**
1900	17²/₃ million	**.40**	1911-S	3¹/₂ million	**.50**
1900-O	2 million	**2.00**	1912	19¹/₃ million	**.35**
1900-S	5¹/₄ million	**.85**	1912-D	11³/₄ million	**.35**
1901	18³/₄ million	**.40**	1912-S	3¹/₂ million	**.35**
1901-O	5²/₃ million	**.85**	1913	19³/₄ million	**.35**
1901-S	593,000	**14.00**	1913-S	510,000	**3.50**
1902	21¹/₃ million	**.40**	1914	17¹/₂ million	**.35**
1902-O	4¹/₂ million	**.85**	1914-D	12 million	**.35**
1902-S	2 million	**1.50**	1914-S	2 million	**.85**
1903	19¹/₂ million	**.40**	1915	5²/₃ million	**.35**
1903-O	8¹/₄ million	**.85**	1915-S	960,000	**.75**
1903-S	613,300	**12.50**	1916	18¹/₂ million	**.30**
1904	14²/₃ million	**.40**	1916-S	5³/₄ million	**.30**
1904-S	800,000	**9.00**			

Type: Mercury head.

(The mint marks are on the bottom of the Rev. to the left of the branches)

Date	Amount Minted	Value	Date	Amount Minted	Value
1916	22¼ million	**1.00**	1931	3¼ million	**.60**
1916-D	264,000	**160.00**	1931-D	1¼ million	**2.00**
1916-S	10½ million	**1.25**	1931-S	1¾ million	**1.00**
1917	55¼ million	**.50**	1934	24 million	**.27**
1917-D	9½ million	**1.25**	1934-D	6¾ million	**.27**
1917-S	27½ million	**.65**	1935	58¾ million	**.27**
1918	26⅔ million	**.70**	1935-D	10½ million	**.27**
1918-D	22⅔ million	**.70**	1935-S	15¾ million	**.27**
1918-S	19½ million	**.60**	1936	87½ million	**.27**
1919	35¾ million	**.60**	1936-D	16¼ million	**.27**
1919-D	10 million	**1.00**	1936-S	9¼ million	**.27**
1919-S	8¾ million	**.75**	1937	56¾ million	**.27**
1920	59 million	**.40**	1937-D	14¼ million	**.27**
1920-D	19¼ million	**.60**	1937-S	9¾ million	**.27**
1920-S	13¾ million	**.50**	1938	22¼ million	**.27**
1921	1¼ million	**8.00**	1938-D	5½ million	**.27**
1921-D	1 million	**13.50**	1938-S	8 million	**.27**
1923	50¼ million	**.30**	1939	67¾ million	**.27**
1923-S	6½ million	**1.00**	1939-D	24½ million	**.27**
1924	24 million	**.60**	1939-S	10½ million	**.27**
1924-D	6¾ million	**.70**	1940	65½ million	**.27**
1924-S	7 million	**.65**	1940-D	21¼ million	**.27**
1925	25⅔ million	**.50**	1940-S	21½ million	**.27**
1925-D	5 million	**1.25**	1941	175 million	**.27**
1925-S	5¾ million	**.60**	1941-D	45⅔ million	**.27**
1926	32¼ million	**.30**	1941-S	43 million	**.27**
1926-D	6¾ million	**.75**	1942	205½ million	**.27**
1926-S	1½ million	**2.50**	1942/1		**75.00**
1927	28 million	**.30**	1942-D	60¾ million	**.27**
1927-D	4¾ million	**.75**	1942-S	49½ million	**.27**
1927-S	4¾ million	**.60**	1943	191¾ million	**.27**
1928	19½ million	**.30**	1943-D	72 million	**.27**
1928-D	4¼ million	**.75**	1943-S	60½ million	**.27**
1928-S	7⅓ million	**.55**	1944	231½ million	**.27**
1929	26 million	**.30**	1944-D	62¼ million	**.27**
1929-D	5 million	**.75**	1944-S	49½ million	**.27**
1929-S	4¾ million	**.40**	1945	159¼ million	**.27**
1930	6¾ million	**.30**	1945-D	40¼ million	**.27**
1930-S	1¾ million	**1.00**	1945-S	42 million	**.27**

*(The valuations in this book are based on the coins
being in G-VG condition, unless otherwise noted.)*

Type: Roosevelt head.

(From 1946–1964, the mint marks are on the Rev., at left bottom of torch.
From 1968 to date, the mint marks are on the obverse above the date.)

Date	Amount Minted	Value	Date	Amount Minted	Value
1946	255¼ million	.27	1967	2¼ billion	.10
1946-D	61 million	.27	1968	424½ million	.10
1946-S	28 million	.27	1968-D	480¾ million	.10
1947	121½ million	.27	1968-S	3 million proofs	.20
1947-D	46¾ million	.27	1969	145¾ million	.10
1947-S	34¾ million	.27	1969-D	563⅓ million	.10
1948	75 million	.27	1969-S	3 million proofs	.20
1948-D	52¾ million	.27	1970	345½ million	.10
1948-S	35½ million	.27	1970-D	755 million	.10
1949	31 million	.27	1970-S	2½ million proofs	.30
1949-D	26 million	.27	1971	162⅔ million	.10
1949-S	13½ million	.40	1971-D	378 million	.10
1950	50¼ million	.27	1971-S	3¼ million	.30
1950-D	46¾ million	.27	1972	431½ million	.10
1950-S	20½ million	.27	1972-D	330¼ million	.10
1951	104 million	.27	1972-S	3¼ million	.30
1951-D	52¼ million	.27	1973	315⅔ million	.10
1951-S	31⅔ million	.27	1973-D	455 million	.10
1952	92¼ million	.27	1973-S	2¾ million	.40
1952-D	122 million	.27	1974	470¼ million	.10
1952-S	44½ million	.27	1974-D	571 million	.10
1953	53⅔ million	.27	1974-S	2⅔ million proofs	.25
1953-D	136½ million	.27	1975	585¾ million	.10
1953-S	39¼ million	.27	1975-D	313¾ million	.10
1954	114¼ million	.27	1975-S	2¾ million proofs	.25
1954-D	106½ million	.27	1976	568¾ million	.10
1954-S	22¾ million	.27	1976-D	695¼ million	.10
1955	12¾ million	.27	1976-S	4¼ million proofs	.20
1955-D	14 million	.27	1977	797 million	.10
1955-S	18½ million	.27	1977-D	376½ million	.10
1956	108¾ million	.27	1977-S	3¼ million proofs	.25
1956-D	108 million	.27	1978	664 million	.10
1957	160¼ million	.27	1978-D	282¾ million	.10
1957-D	113⅓ million	.27	1978-S	3¼ million proofs	.25
1958	32 million	.27	1979	315½ million	.10
1958-D	136½ million	.27	1979-D	391 million	.10
1959	85¾ million	.27	1979-S	3¾ million proofs	.25
1959-D	165 million	.27	1980	73.5 million	.10
1960	72 million	.27	1980-D	719⅓ million	.10
1960-D	200¼ million	.27	1980-S	3½ million proofs	.30
1961	93¾ million	.27	1981	676⅔ million	.10
1961-D	209¼ million	.27	1981-S	712¼ million	.10
1962	72½ million	.27	1981-S	4 million proofs	.25
1962-D	353¼ million	.27	1982	519½ million	.10
1963	123⅔ million	.27	1982-D	542¾ million	.10
1963-D	421½ million	.27	1982-S	3¾ million proofs	.25
1964	929⅓ million	.27	1983	647 million	.10
1964-D	1⅓ billion	.27	1983-D	730 million	.10
			1983-S	3¾ million proofs	.50
	CLAD COINAGE		1984	856¼ million	.10
			1984-D	700 million	.10
1965	1⅔ billion	.10	1984-S	3 million proofs	.50
1966	1⅓ billion	.10			

Date	Amount Minted	Value	Date	Amount Minted	Value
1985	705 million	.10	1990-S	proofs	.60
1985-D	588 million	.10	1991	827.2 million	.10
1985-S	3.4 million proofs		1991-D	601.2 million	.10
1986	683 million	.10	1991-S	2.87 million proofs	.60
1986-D	473 million	.10	1992	593.5 million	.10
1986-S	3 million proofs	.50	1992-D	616.3 million	.10
1987	763 million	.10	1992-S	2.86 million proofs	.50
1987-D	653 million	.10	1992-S	1.3 million 90% silver proof	1.50
1987-S	3¾ million proofs	.35	1993	766.2 million	.10
1988	1 billion	.10	1993-D	750.1 million	.10
1988-D	962⅓ million	.10	1993-S	26.3 million proofs	.50
1988-S	3.23 million proofs	1.40	1993-S	761.3 million silver proofs	1.00
1989	3 billion	.10	1994		.10
1989-D	896.5 million	.10	1994-D		.10
1989-S	3.22 million proofs	1.50	1994-S	proofs	.50
1990	1 billion	.10	1994-S	silver proofs	1.00
1990-D	840 million	.10			

20 CENT PIECES

Type: Liberty seated.

(The mint marks are on the Rev., under the eagle)

Date	Amount Minted	Value	Date	Amount Minted	Value
1875	39,700	25.00	1876-CC	10,000*	Rare
1875-S	1⅛ million	20.00	1877	510 proofs	1,200.00
1875-CC	133,300	27.00	1878	600 proofs	1,000.00
1876	15,900	40.00	*About a dozen are actually known.		

QUARTERS

Type: Draped bust of Liberty; small eagle on Rev.

Date	Amount Minted	Value
1796	5.900	2,500.00

Type: Draped bust of Liberty; large eagle on Rev.

Date	Amount Minted	Value	Date	Amount Minted	Value
1804	6,700	**500.00**	1806	206,100	**100.00**
1805	121,400	**100.00**	1807	220,600	**100.00**

Type: Bust of Liberty wearing cap; motto over the eagle.

Date	Amount Minted	Value	Date	Amount Minted	Value
1815	69,200	**20.00**	1823	17,800	**3,000.00**
1818	361,200	**18.00**	1824	Unknown	**35.00**
1819	144,000	**20.00**	1825	168,000	**18.00**
1820	127,400	**20.00**	1827	4,000	**Rare**
1821	216,900	**18.00**	1828	102,000	**18.00**
1822	64,000	**30.00**			

Type: Bust of Liberty wearing cap; without motto over the eagle.

Date	Amount Minted	Value	Date	Amount Minted	Value
1831	398,000	**17.50**	1835	2 million	**17.50**
1832	320,000	**17.50**	1836	472,000	**17.50**
1833	156,000	**22.50**	1837	252,400	**17.50**
1834	286,000	**17.50**	1838	Part of 832,000	**17.50**

Without arrows or rays
1838–1853 & 1856–1865

With arrows and rays 1853 only
With arrows only, 1854–1855

Type: Liberty seated; without motto over the eagle.

(The mint marks are on the Rev., under the eagle)

Date	Amount Minted	Value	Date	Amount Minted	Value
1838	Part of 832,000	4.50	1854	12½ million	3.00
1839	491,000	4.00	1854-O	1½ million	3.50
1840	188,127	9.00	1855	2¾ million	3.50
1840-O	425,200	5.00	1855-O	176,000	12.50
1840-O w/Drapery		7.50	1855-S	396,400	12.00
1841	120,000	20.00	1856	7¼ million	3.00
1841-O	452,000	8.00	1856-O	968,000	4.00
1842	88,000	30.00	1856-S	286,000	15.00
1842-O	769,000	5.00	1857	9⅔ million	3.50
1843	645,600	3.25	1857-O	1¼ million	4.00
1843-O	968,000	5.25	1857-S	82,000	25.00
1844	421,200	3.50	1858	7⅓ million	3.00
1844-O	740,000	3.50	1858-O	520,000	4.00
1845	922,000	3.25	1858-S	121,000	20.00
1846	510,000	4.00	1859	1⅓ million	3.50
1847	734,000	3.25	1859-O	260,000	5.00
1847-O	368,000	7.50	1859-S	80,000	35.00
1848	146,000	10.00	1860	805,400	3.50
1849	340,000	5.00	1860-O	388,000	4.00
1849-O	Unknown	185.00	1860-S	56,000	50.00
1850	190,800	12.00	1861	4¾ million	3.50
1850-O	412,000	8.00	1861-S	96,000	24.00
1851	160,000	12.50	1862	932,600	3.60
1851-O	88,000	75.00	1862-S	67,000	25.00
1852	177,100	15.00	1863	192,100	12.50
1852-O	96,000	65.00	1864	94,100	20.00
1853 Arr. & Rays	15¼ million	3.50	1864-S	20,000	75.00
1853/3 No Arr.	Part of above	75.00	1865	59,300	20.00
1853-O	1½ million	3.50	1865-S	41,000	30.00

Without arrows at date
1866–1873 & 1875–1891

With arrows at date
1873–1874

Type: Liberty seated; with motto over the eagle.

(The mint marks are on the Rev., under the eagle)

Date	Amount Minted	Value	Date	Amount Minted	Value
1866	17,500	80.00	1876	17³/₄ million	3.00
1866-S	28,000	70.00	1876-S	8¹/₂ million	3.00
1867	20,600	55.00	1876-CC	5 million	4.00
1867-S	48,000	35.00	1877	11 million	3.00
1868	30,000	35.00	1877-S	9 million	3.00
1868-S	96,000	20.00	1877-CC	4¹/₄ million	3.00
1869	16,600	80.00	1878	2¹/₄ million	3.00
1869-S	76,000	27.50	1878-S	140,000	25.00
1870	87,400	15.00	1878-CC	996,000	7.50
1870-CC	8,300	800.00	1879	14,700	50.00
1871	171,200	12.50	1880	15,000	50.00
1871-S	30,900	80.00	1881	13,000	50.00
1871-CC	10,900	400.00	1882	16,300	50.00
1872	182,900	10.00	1883	15,400	50.00
1872-S	83,000	125.00	1884	8,900	60.00
1872-CC	9,100	110.00	1885	14,500	50.00
1873-No Arr.	143,700	12.00	1886	5,900	125.00
1873-CC-No Arr.	4,000	Rare	1887	10,700	100.00
1873-Arr.	1¹/₂ million	4.00	1888	10,800	50.00
1873-S.Arr.	156,000	8.00	1888-S	1¹/₄ million	3.00
1873-CC-Arr.	12,500	475.00	1889	12,700	50.00
1874	471,900	5.00	1890	80,600	20.00
1874-S	392,000	6.00	1891	4 million	3.00
1875	4¹/₄ million	3.00	1891-O	68,000	50.00
1875-S	680,000	10.00	1891-S	2¹/₄ million	3.00
1875-CC	140,000	22.00			

*(The valuations in this book are based on the coins
being in G-VG condition, unless otherwise noted.)*

Type: Liberty head.
(The mint marks are on the Rev., under the eagle)

Date	Amount Minted	Value	Date	Amount Minted	Value
1892	8¼ million	1.25	1904-O	2½ million	1.90
1892-O	2⅔ million	2.25	1905	5 million	1.50
1892-S	964,100	6.00	1905-O	1¼ million	2.00
1893	5½ million	1.25	1905-S	1¾ million	2.25
1893-O	3½ million	1.50	1906	3⅔ million	1.25
1893-S	1½ million	2.00	1906-D	3⅓ million	1.25
1894	3½ million	1.50	1906-O	2 million	1.25
1894-O	2¾ million	1.75	1907	7¼ million	1.25
1894-S	2⅔ million	1.75	1907-D	2½ million	1.25
1895	4½ million	1.25	1907-O	4½ million	1.25
1895-O	2¾ million	1.75	1907-S	1⅓ million	1.50
1895-S	1¾ million	1.90	1908	4¼ million	1.50
1896	3¾ million	1.50	1908-D	5¾ million	1.50
1896-O	1½ million	2.00	1908-O	6¼ million	1.50
1896-S	188,000	90.00	1908-S	784,000	3.00
1897	8 million	1.50	1909	9¼ million	1.50
1897-O	1½ million	3.00	1909-D	5 million	1.50
1897-S	542,200	4.00	1909-O	712,000	3.00
1898	1 million	1.50	1909-S	1⅓ million	1.50
1898-O	1¾ million	2.00	1910	2¼ million	1.50
1898-S	1 million	2.00	1910-D	1½ million	1.50
1899	12⅔ million	1.50	1911	3¾ million	1.50
1899-O	2⅔ million	1.90	1911-D	933,600	1.50
1899-S	708,000	3.00	1911-S	988,000	1.50
1900	10 million	1.50	1912	4½ million	1.50
1900-O	3½ million	2.25	1912-S	708,000	1.50
1900-S	1¾ million	2.25	1913	484,600	4.50
1901	9 million	1.50	1913-D	1½ million	1.50
1901-O	1⅔ million	6.00	1913-S	40,000	200.00
1901-S	72,700	750.00	1914	6¼ million	1.50
1902	12¼ million	1.50	1914-D	3 million	1.50
1902-O	4¾ million	1.90	1914-S	264,000	22.50
1902-S	1½ million	3.50	1915	3½ million	1.50
1903	9⅔ million	1.50	1915-D	3¾ million	1.50
1903-O	3½ million	1.90	1915-S	704,000	1.90
1903-S	1 million	3.25	1916	1¾ million	1.50
1904	9½ million	1.25	1916-D	6½ million	1.50

Type I. No stars under eagle
1916–1917

Type II. Three stars under eagle
1917–1930

Type: Liberty standing

(The mint marks are on the Obv., above and to left of the date)

Date	Amount Minted	Average Circulated	Extra Fine
1916	52,000	500.00	2,000.00
1917T.I	8¾ million	4.00	25.00
1917-DT.I	1½ million	5.00	35.00
1917-ST.I	2 million	5.50	55.00
1917T.II	14 million	5.00	15.00
1917-DT.II	6¼ million	7.50	37.50
1917-ST.II	5½ million	6.50	30.00
1918	14¼ million	6.00	20.00
1918-D	7⅓ million	10.00	37.50
1918-S	11 million	7.00	25.00
1918-S over 17	—	550.00	3,000.00
1919	11⅓ million	11.00	32.00
1919-D	2 million	22.50	125.00
1919-S	1¾ million	22.50	185.00
1920	28 million	7.50	20.00
1920-D	3½ million	10.00	45.00
1920-S	6½ million	8.00	25.00
1921	2 million	27.50	120.00
1923	9¾ million	6.00	15.00
1923-S	1⅓ million	40.00	200.00
1924	11 million	7.00	14.00
1924-D	3 million	12.00	37.00
1924-S	3 million	8.00	35.00
1925	12¼ million	1.00	12.00
1926	11¼ million	1.00	12.00
1926-D	1¾ million	2.50	18.00
1926-S	2¾ million	1.25	45.00
1927	12 million	1.00	12.00
1927-D	976,400	2.00	40.00
1927-S	396,000	2.00	550.00
1928	6⅓ million	1.00	12.00
1928-D	1⅔ million	1.50	16.00
1928-S	2⅔ million	1.00	14.00
1929	11 million	1.00	12.00
1929-D	1⅓ million	1.75	15.00
1929-S	1¾ million	1.00	12.50
1930	5⅔ million	1.00	12.00
1930-S	1⅔ million	1.00	12.00

Reg. Obv.	Reg. Rev.	Bicentennial	Bicentennial
1932–1974	1932–1974	Obv.—1976	Rev.—1976

Type: Washington head

(From 1932–1964, the mint marks are on the Rev., under the eagle.
From 1968 to date, the mint marks are on the obverse, to the right of Washington's neck)

Date	Amount Minted	Value	Date	Amount Minted	Value
1932	5½ million	.75	1949	9⅓ million	.65
1932-D	436,800	20.00	1949-D	10 million	.65
1932-S	408,000	17.50	1950	25 million	.65
1934	32 million	.65	1950-D	21 million	.65
1934-D	3½ million	2.00	1950-S	10⅓ million	.65
1935	32½ million	.65	1951	43½ million	.65
1935-D	5¾ million	.75	1951-D	35½ million	.65
1935-S	5¾ million	.75	1951-S	9 million	.65
1936	41⅓ million	.65	1952	39 million	.65
1936-D	5½ million	1.00	1952-D	49¾ million	.65
1936-S	3¾ million	.75	1952-S	13¾ million	.65
1937	19¾ million	.65	1953	18¾ million	.65
1937-D	7¼ million	1.00	1953-D	56 million	.65
1937-S	1¾ million	1.25	1953-S	14 million	.65
1938	9½ million	.70	1954	54⅔ million	.65
1938-S	2¾ million	1.00	1954-D	46⅓ million	.65
1939	33½ million	.65	1954-S	11¾ million	.65
1939-D	7 million	.65	1955	18⅔ million	.65
1939-S	2⅔ million	1.00	1955-D	3¼ million	.65
1940	35¾ million	.65	1956	44¼ million	.65
1940-D	2¾ million	.65	1956-D	32½ million	.65
1940-S	8¼ million	.65	1957	46½ million	.65
1941	79 million	.65	1957-D	78 million	.65
1941-D	16¾ million	.65	1958	6⅓ million	.65
1941-S	16 million	.65	1958-D	78¼ million	.65
1942	102 million	.65	1959	24⅓ million	.65
1942-D	17½ million	.65	1959-D	62 million	.65
1942-S	19½ million	.65	1960	30¾ million	.65
1943	99¾ million	.65	1960-D	63 million	.65
1943-D	16 million	.65	1961	37 million	.65
1943-S	21¾ million	.65	1961-D	80¼ million	.65
1944	105 million	.65	1962	36¼ million	.65
1944-D	14⅔ million	.65	1962-D	127½ million	.65
1944-S	12⅔ million	.65	1963	74⅓ million	.65
1945	74½ million	.65	1963-D	135¼ million	.65
1945-D	12⅓ million	.65	1964	560⅓ million	.65
1945-S	17 million	.65	1964-D	704 million	.65
1946	53½ million	.65	**CLAD COINAGE**		
1946-D	9 million	.65	1965	1¾ billion	.25
1946-S	4¼ million	.65	1966	821 million	.25
1947	22⅔ million	.65	1967	11.12 billion	.25
1947-D	15⅓ million	.65	1968	220¾ million	.25
1947-S	5½ million	.65	1968-D	101½ million	.25
1948	35¼ million proofs	.65	1968-S	3 million proofs	.30
1948-D	16¾ million	.65	1969	176¼ million	.25
1948-S	16 million	.65	1969-D	114⅓ million	.25

Date	Amount Minted	Value	Date	Amount Minted	Value
1969-S	3 million proofs	.35	1983	673½ million	1.00
1970	136½ million	.25	1983-D	618 million	1.50
1970-D	417⅓ million	.25	1983-S	3.8 million proofs	.60
1970-S	2½ million proofs	.35	1984	673½ million	.25
1971-D	258⅔ million	.25	1984-D	546½ million	.25
1971-S	3¼ million proofs	.35	1984-S	3 million proofs	.50
1971	109¼ million	.25	1985	776 million	.25
1972	215 million	.25	1985-D	520 million	.25
1972-D	311 million	.25	1985-S	3.4 million proofs	.50
1972-S	3¼ million proofs	.35	1986	551 million	.25
1973	347 million	.25	1986-D	504 million	.25
1973-D	233 million	.25	1986-S	3 million proofs	.60
1973-S	2¾ million proofs	.30	1987	582½ million	.25
1974	801½ million	.25	1987-D	655½ million	.25
1974-D	353¼ million	.25	1987-S	3¾ million proofs	.30
1974-S	2⅔ million proofs	.30	1988	562 million	.25
1975	none minted	—	1988-D	600 million	.25
1976	809¾ million	.25	1988-S	3.23 million proofs	.40
1976-D	860 million	.25	1989	512.8 million	.25
1976-S	cupro-nickel, proof, 7 million	.30	1989-D	896.7 million	.25
1976-S	silver	.60	1989-S	3.22 million proofs	.50
1976-S	silver, proof	1.00	1990	613.8 million	.25
1977	468½ million	.25	1990-D	927.6 million	.25
1977-D	256½ million	.25	1990-S	3.3 million proofs	.50
1977-S	3¼ million proofs	.30	1991	571 million	.25
1978	521½ million	.25	1991-D	691 million	.25
1978-D	287¼ million	.25	1991-S	2.87 million proof	.60
1978-S	3¼ million proofs	.30	1992	384.8 million	.25
1979	515¾ million	.25	1992-D	389.8 million	.25
1979-D	489¾ million	.25	1992-S	2.86 million proof	1.00
1979-S	3¾ million proofs	.30	1992-S	1.3 million 90% silver proof	2.75
1980	635¾ million	.25	1993	639.3 million	.25
1980-D	518⅓ million	.25	1993-D	645.5 million	.25
1980-S	3½ million proofs	.30	1993-S	2.6 million proofs	1.00
1981	601¾ million	.25	1993-S	1.3 million silver proofs	2.00
1981-D	575¾ million	.25	1994		.25
1981-S	4 million proofs	.30	1994-D		.25
1982	501 million	1.00	1994-S	proofs	1.00
1982-D	480 million	.25	1994-S	silver proofs	2.00
1982-S	3.8 million proofs	.60			

HALF DOLLARS

Type: Liberty head with flowing hair.

Date	Amount Minted	Value	Date	Amount Minted	Value
1794	5,300	**500.00**	1795	317,800	**225.00**

Type: Draped bust of Liberty; small eagle on Rev.

Date	Amount Minted	Value	Date	Amount Minted	Value
1796	Unknown	**4,500.00**	1797		**4,500.00**

Type: Draped bust of Liberty; large eagle on Rev.

Date	Amount Minted	Value	Date	Amount Minted	Value
1801	30,300	**85.00**	1805	211,700	**50.00**
1802	29,900	**70.00**	1806	839,600	**50.00**
1803	31,700	**65.00**	1807	301,100	**50.00**

*(The valuations in this book are based on the coins
being in G-VG condition, unless otherwise noted.)*

Type: Bust of Liberty wearing cap; motto over eagle lettered edge; large size.

Date	Amount Minted	Value	Date	Amount Minted	Value
1807	750,500	**22.00**	1823	1²/₃ million	**15.00**
1808	1¹/₂ million	**18.00**	1824	3¹/₂ million	**15.00**
1809	1¹/₂ million	**18.00**	1825	3 million	**15.00**
1810	1¹/₄ million	**17.50**	1826	4 million	**15.00**
1811	1¹/₄ million	**17.50**	1827	5¹/₂ million	**15.00**
1812	1²/₃ million	**17.50**	1828	3 million	**15.00**
1813	1¹/₄ million	**17.50**	1829	3³/₄ million	**15.00**
1814	1 million	**17.50**	1830	4³/₄ million	**15.00**
1815	47,100	**350.00**	1831	5³/₄ million	**15.00**
1817	1¹/₄ million	**15.00**	1832	4³/₄ million	**15.00**
1818	2 million	**15.00**	1833	5¹/₄ million	**15.00**
1819	2¹/₄ million	**15.00**	1834	6¹/₃ million	**15.00**
1820	751,100	**17.50**	1835	5¹/₃ million	**15.00**
1821	1¹/₃ million	**17.00**	1836	Part of 6¹/₂ million	**15.00**
1822	1¹/₂ million	**17.00**			

Type: Bust of Liberty wearing cap; no motto over eagle; reeded edge; reduced size; value expressed as "50 cents."

Date	Amount Minted	Value	Date	Amount Minted	Value
1836	Part of 6¹/₂ million	**450.00**	1837	3²/₃ million	**17.50**

Type: Same as above; but value is expressed as "Half Dot."

(The mint marks are on the Obv., over the date)

Date	Amount Minted	Value	Date	Amount Minted	Value
1838	3½ million	**16.00**	1839	Part of 3½ million	**16.00**
1838-O	About 20	**Rare**	1839-O	163,000	**50.00**

Without arrows or rays, 1839–1853 & 1856–1866
With arrows and rays, 1853 only
With arrows only, 1854–1855

Type: Liberty seated; without motto over the eagle.

(The mint marks are on the Rev., under the eagle)

Date	Amount Minted	Value	Date	Amount Minted	Value
1839	Part of 3⅓ million	**15.00**	1852	77,100	**125.00**
1840	1½ million	**7.50**	1852-O	144,000	**20.00**
1840-O	855,100	**11.00**	1853-Arr. & Rays	3½ million	**8.00**
1841	310,000	**15.00**	1853-O-No Arr. & Rays	1½ million	**Rare**
1841-O	401,000	**7.50**	1853-O-Arr. & Rays	Part of above	**8.00**
1842	2 million	**6.00**	1854	3 million	**7.00**
1842-O	957,000	**6.00**	1854-O	5¼ million	**7.00**
1843	3¾ million	**6.00**	1855	759,500	**9.00**
1843-O	2¼ million	**6.00**	1855-O	3⅔ million	**6.00.**
1844	1¾ million	**6.00**	1855-S	129,900	**150.00**
1844-O	2 million	**6.00**	1856	938,000	**7.00**
1845	589,000	**12.50**	1856-O	2⅔ million	**6.00**
1845-O	2 million	**6.00**	1856-S	211,000	**12.00**
1846	2¼ million	**6.00**	1857	2 million	**6.00**
1846-O	2⅓ million	**6.00**	1857-O	818,000	**6.00**
1847	1¼ million	**6.00**	1857-S	158,000	**20.00**
1847-O	2½ million	**6.00**	1858	4¼ million	**6.00**
1848	580,000	**12.50**	1858-O	7¼ million	**6.00**
1848-O	3¼ million	**7.00**	1858-S	476,000	**9.00**
1849	1¼ million	**9.00**	1859	748,000	**6.00**
1849-O	2⅓ million	**7.00**	1859-O	2¾ million	**6.00**
1850	227,000	**100.00**	1859-S	566,000	**9.00**
1850-O	2½ million	**7.00**	1860	303,700	**9.00**
1851	200,700	**110.00**	1860-O	1¼ million	**6.00**
1851-O	402,000	**12.00**	1860-S	472,000	**8.00**

Date	Amount Minted	Value	Date	Amount Minted	Value
1861	2³/₄ million	6.00	1863-S	916,000	6.00
1861-O	2¹/₂ million	6.00	1864	379,600	10.00
1861-S	939,500	6.00	1864-S	658,000	6.00
1862	252,300	10.00	1865	11,900	9.00
1862-S	1¹/₃ million	6.00	1865-S	675,000	6.00
1863	503,700	8.00	1866-S	Part of 1 million	40.00

Without arrows at date, 1866–1873 & 1875–1891. With arrows at date, 1873–1874

Type: Liberty seated; with motto over the eagle.

(The mint marks are on the Rev., under the eagle)

Date	Amount Minted	Value	Date	Amount Minted	Value
1866	745,600	6.00	1875	6 million	6.00
1866-S	Part of 1 million	6.00	1875-S	3¹/₄ million	6.00
1867	424,300	7.00	1875-CC	1 million	7.00
1867-S	1¹/₄ million	6.00	1876	8¹/₂ million	6.00
1868	378,200	15.00	1876-S	4¹/₂ million	6.00
1868-S	1¹/₄ million	6.00	1876-CC	2 million	7.00
1869	795,900	7.00	1877	8¹/₂ million	5.00
1869-S	656,000	6.00	1877-S	5¹/₂ million	6.00
1870	600,900	8.00	1877-CC	1¹/₂ million	7.00
1870-S	1 million	6.00	1878	1¹/₂ million	8.00
1870-CC	54,600	225.00	1878-S	12,000	4,000.00
1871	1¹/₄ million	8.00	1878-CC	62,000	150.00
1871-S	2¹/₄ million	6.00	1879	5,900	90.00
1871-CC	139,900	55.00	1880	9,800	70.00
1872	881,500	6.00	1881	11,000	70.00
1872-S	580,000	10.00	1882	5,500	90.00
1872-CC	272,000	25.00	1883	9,000	70.00
1873-No Arr.	820,800	6.00	1884	5,300	90.00
1873-CC-No Arr.	122,500	35.00	1885	6,100	90.00
1873-Arr.	1³/₄ million	9.00	1886	5,900	95.00
1873-S-Arr.	228,000	15.00	1887	5,700	125.00
1873-CC-Arr.	214,600	35.00	1888	12,800	75.00
1874	2¹/₃ million	9.00	1889	12,700	75.00
1874-S	394,000	15.00	1890	12,600	75.00
1874-CC	59,000	95.00	1891	200,600	15.00

Type: Liberty Head.

(The mint marks are on the Rev., under the eagle)

Date	Amount Minted	Value	Date	Amount Minted	Value
1892	1 million	8.00	1904-O	1 million	4.00
1892-O	390,000	35.00	1904-S	553,000	5.00
1892-S	1 million	40.00	1905	663,000	4.50
1893	1¾ million	4.00	1905-O	505,000	5.00
1893-O	1 ½ million	7.00	1905-S	2½ million	3.00
1893-S	740,000	25.00	1906	2½ million	2.50
1894	1¼ million	8.00	1906-D	4 million	2.50
1894-O	2¼ million	5.00	1906-O	2½ million	2.50
1894-S	4 million	4.00	1906-S	1¾ million	2.50
1895	1¾ million	4.00	1907	2½ million	2.50
1895-O	1¾ million	4.00	1907-D	3¾ million	2.50
1895-S	1 million	6.00	1907-O	4 million	2.50
1896	950,800	7.50	1907-S	1¼ million	2.50
1896-O	924,000	7.50	1908	1½ million	2.50
1896-S	1¼ million	24.00	1908-D	3½ million	2.50
1897	2½ million	2.50	1908-O	5½ million	2.50
1897-O	632,000	25.00	1908-S	1⅔ million	2.50
1897-S	933,900	40.00	1909	2½ million	2.50
1898	3 million	2.50	1909-O	925,000	3.50
1898-O	874,000	6.00	1909-S	1¾ million	2.50
1898-S	2½ million	3.75	1910	419,000	4.00
1899	5½ million	2.50	1910-S	2 million	2.50
1899-O	1¾ million	3.75	1911	1½ million	2.50
1899-S	1 ½ million	3.75	1911-D	695,000	2.50
1900	4¾ million	2.50	1911-S	1¼ million	2.50
1900-O	2¾ million	3.75	1912	1½ million	2.50
1900-S	2½ million	3.75	1912-D	2½ million	2.50
1901	4¼ million	2.50	1912-S	1½ million	2.50
1901-O	1 million	3.75	1913	189,000	7.00
1901-S	847,000	5.00	1913-D	534,000	2.50
1902	5 million	2.50	1913-S	604,000	2.50
1902-O	2½ million	3.75	1914	125,000	10.00
1902-S	1½ million	3.75	1914-S	1 million	2.50
1903	2¼ million	3.00	1915	138,000	8.00
1903-O	2 million	2.50	1915-D	1¼ million	2.50
1903-S	2 million	2.50	1915-S	1⅔ million	2.50
1904	3 million	2.50			

Type: Liberty Walking.

(Mint marks: on the coins of 1916 and the early coinage of 1917, the mint marks are on the Obv., under the motto. On the later coinage of 1917 and thereafter, the mint marks are on the Rev., to the left of "Half Dollar.")

Date	Amount Minted	Average Circulated	Extra Fine
1916	608,000	9.00	100.00
1916-D	1 million	5.00	75.00
1916-S	508,000	24.00	325.00
1917	12¼ million	2.00	18.50
1917-D (Obv.)	765,000	5.00	90.00
1917-D (Rev.)	2 million	3.75	90.00
1917-S (Obv.)	1 million	6.50	400.00
1917-S (Rev.)	5½ million	4.00	30.00
1918	6⅔ million	2.50	70.00
1918-D	3¾ million	3.00	80.50
1918-S	10¼ million	2.50	30.00
1919	962,000	5.00	250.00
1919-D	1¼ million	4.00	300.00
1919-S	1½ million	4.00	350.00
1920	6½ million	2.50	30.00
1920-D	1½ million	5.00	200.00
1920-S	4⅔ million	3.00	90.00
1921	246,000	27.50	950.00
1921-D	208,000	37.50	1,500.00
1921-S	548,000	9.50	3,500.00
1923-S	2¼ million	4.00	125.00
1927-S	2½ million	2.50	50.00
1928-S	2 million	2.50	60.00
1929-D	1 million	3.50	40.00
1929-S	2 million	2.50	42.50
1933-S	1¾ million	3.00	30.00
1934	7 million	1.35	4.00
1934-D	2½ million	1.50	15.00
1934-S	3⅔ million	1.50	15.00
1935	9¼ million	1.35	3.50
1935-D	3 million	1.35	13.00
1935-S	3¾ million	1.35	13.00
1936	12½ million	1.35	3.50
1936-D	4¼ million	1.35	9.00
1936-S	4 million	1.35	9.00
1937	9½ million	1.35	3.50
1937-D	1¾ million	1.35	45.00
1937-S	2 million	1.35	25.00
1938	4 million	1.35	4.00
1938-D	491,600	8.50	60.00
1939	6¾ million	1.35	8.00
1939-D	4¼ million	1.35	9.00
1939-S	2½ million	1.35	15.00
1940	9¼ million	1.35	5.00

1940-S	4½ million	**1.35**	**8.00**
1941	24¼ million	**1.35**	**3.00**
1941-D	11¼ million	**1.35**	**2.00**
1941-S	8 million	**1.35**	**3.00**
1942	47¾ million	**1.35**	**2.00**
1942-D	11 million	**1.35**	**2.25**
1942-S	12¾ million	**1.35**	**2.50**
1943	53¼ million	**1.35**	**2.00**
1943-D	11½ million	**1.35**	**2.25**
1943-S	13½ million	**1.35**	**2.25**
1944	28¼ million	**1.35**	**2.00**
1944-D	9¾ million	**1.35**	**2.25**
1944-S	9 million	**1.35**	**2.25**
1945	31½ million	**1.35**	**2.00**
1945-D	10 million	**1.35**	**2.25**
1945-S	10¼ million	**1.35**	**2.25**
1946	12 million	**1.35**	**2.00**
1946-D	2¼ million	**1.75**	**3.50**
1946-S	3¾ million	**1.35**	**2.00**
1947	4 million	**1.35**	**7.00**
1947-D	4 million	**1.35**	**7.00**

Type: Franklin Head.

(The mint marks are on the Rev., above the Liberty Bell)

Date	Amount Minted	Value	Date	Amount Minted	Value
1948	3 million	**1.35**	1954-S	5 million	**1.35**
1948-D	4 million	**1.35**	1955	3 million	**1.35**
1949	5¾ million	**1.35**	1956	4¼ million	**1.35**
1949-D	4 million	**1.35**	1957	5 million	**1.35**
1949-S	3¾ million	**1.75**	1957-D	20 million	**1.35**
1950	7¾ million	**1.35**	1958	4 million	**1.35**
1950-D	8 million	**1.35**	1958-D	24 million	**1.35**
1951	16¾ million	**1.35**	1959	6¼ million	**1.35**
1951-D	9½ million	**1.35**	1959-D	13 million	**1.35**
1951-S	13⅔ million	**1.35**	1960	7¾ million	**1.35**
1952	21¼ million	**1.35**	1960-D	18¼ million	**1.35**
1952-D	25½ million	**1.35**	1961	8¼ million	**1.35**
1952-S	5½ million	**1.35**	1961-D	20¼ million	**1.35**
1953	2¾ million	**1.75**	1962	9¾ million	**1.35**
1953-D	21 million	**1.15**	1962-D	35½ million	**1.35**
1953-S	4¼ million	**1.50**	1963	22 million	**1.35**
1954	13½ million	**1.35**	1963-D	67 million	**1.35**
1954-D	24½ million	**1.35**			

Reg. Obv.
1964–1974

Reg. Rev.
1964–1974

Bicentennial
Obv.—1976

Bicentennial
Rev.—1976

Type: Kennedy Head

(In 1964 the mint mark is on the Rev., under the eagle's right talon
From 1968 to date, the mint marks are on the obverse, just below the base of Kennedy's neck)

Date	Amount Minted	Value	Date	Amount Minted	Value
	SILVER		1980-S	3½ million proofs	.5
1964	277¼ million	1.15	1981	29½ million	.50
1964-D	156¼ million	1.15	1981-D	27¾ million	.50
	SILVER CLAD		1981-S	4 million proofs	.5
			1982	10.8 million	.50
1965	65¾ million	.55	1982-D	13 million	.50
1966	109 million	.55	1982-S	3.8 million proofs	1.25
1967	295 million	.55	1983	34 million	.50
1968-D	247 million	.55	1983-D	32½ million	.50
1968-S	3 million proofs	1.00	1983-S	3.8 million proofs	.75
1969-D	129¾ million	.55	1984	26 million	.50
1969-S	3 million proofs	1.00	1984-D	26¼ million	.50
1970-D	2¼ million	8.00	1984-S	3 million proofs	2.00
1970-S	2½ million proofs	3.00	1985	18.7 million	.50
			1985-D	19.8 million	.50
	COPPER-NICKEL CLAD		1985-S	3.4 million proofs	2.00
1971	155¼ million	.50	1986	13.1 million	.50
1971-D	302 million	.50	1986-D	15.3 million	.50
1971-S	3¼ million proofs	.90	1986-S	3 million proofs	5.00
1972	153 million	.50	1987	2.9 million	.50
1972-D	141¾ million	.50	1987-D	2.9 million	.50
1972-S	3¼ million proofs	1.00	1987-S	3¾ million proofs	1.00
1973	65 million	.50	1988	13.6 million	.50
1973-D	83 million	.50	1988-D	12 million	.50
1973-S	2¾ million proofs	1.00	1988-S	3.23 million proofs	3.50
1974	201½ million	.50	1989	24.5 million	.50
1974-D	79 million	.50	1989-D	23 million	.50
1974-S	2⅔ million proofs	1.00	1989-S	3.22 million proofs	1.00
1975	none minted		1990	22.28 million	.50
1976	234½ million	.50	1990-D	20.1 million	.50
1976-D	287½ million	.50	1990-S	proofs	1.25
1976-S	cupro-nickel, proof		1991	14.8 million	.50
	7 million	1.00	1991-D	15 million	.50
1976-S	silver	1.25	1991-S	2.87 million proof	4.00
1976-S	silver, proof	1.75	1992	17.6 million	.50
1977	43½ million	.50	1992-D	17 million	.50
1977-D	3½ million	.50	1992-S	2.86 million proofs	3.00
1977-S	3¼ million proofs	.75	1992-S	1.3 million 90% silver pfoof	7.00
1978	14⅓ million	.50	1993	15.5 million	.50
1978-D	13¾ million	.50	1993-D	15 million	.50
1978-S	3¼ million proofs	.75	1993-S	2.63 million proofs	3.00
1979	68⅓ million	.50	1993-S	761.353 silver proofs	6.00
1979-D	15¾ million	.50	1994		
1979-S	3¾ million proofs	.85	1994-D		
1980	44 million	.50	1994-S	proofs	
1980-D	33½million	.50	1994-S	silver proofs	

SILVER DOLLARS

Type: Head of Liberty with flowing hair.

Date	Amount Minted	Value	Date	Amount Minted	Value
1794	1,758	**4,000.00**	1795	Part of 184,000	**450.00**

Type: Draped bust of Liberty; with small eagle on Rev.

Date	Amount Minted	Value	Date	Amount Minted	Value
1795	Part of 184,000	**300.00**	1797	7,800	**300.00**
1796	72,900	**300.00**	1798	Part of 327,500	**400.00**

Type: Draped bust of Liberty; with large eagle on Rev.

Date	Amount Minted	Value	Date	Amount Minted	Value
1798	Part of 327,500	**175.00**	1802	41,600	**175.00**
1799	423,500	**175.00**	1803	66,100	**200.00**
1800	220,900	**175.00**	1804	——	——
1801	54,500	**200.00**		(less than 15 specimens are known of the 1804 Dollar.)	

Type: Liberty seated; with flying eagle on Rev.—the Gobrecht design.

Date	Amount Minted	Value	Date	Amount Minted	Value
1836	About 1,000	**1,000.00**	1839	About 300	**1,300.00**
1838	About 100	**2,000.00**			

Type: Liberty seated; without motto over the eagle.
(The mint marks are on the Rev., under the eagle)

Date	Amount Minted	Value	Date	Amount Minted	Value
1840	61,000	**75.00**	1854	33,100	**500.00**
1841	173,000	**45.00**	1855	26,000	**300.00**
1842	184,600	**45.00**	1856	63,500	**90.00**
1843	165,100	**45.00**	1857	94,000	**90.00**
1844	20,000	**100.00**	1858	Proof, About 100	**3,000.00**
1845	24,500	**75.00**	1859	256,500	**90.00**
1846	110,600	**40.00**	1859-O	360,000	**40.00**
1846-O	59,000	**50.00**	1859-S	20,000	**80.00**
1847	140,700	**45.00**	1860	218,900	**70.00**
1848	15,000	**100.00**	1860-O	515,000	**40.00**
1849	62,600	**40.00**	1861	78,500	**175.00**
1850	7,500	**175.00**	1862	12,100	**125.00**
1850-O	40,000	**90.00**	1863	27,700	**100.00**
1851	1,300	**Rare**	1864	31,200	**90.00**
1852	1,100	**Rare**	1865	47,000	**90.00**
1853	46,100	**75.00**			

Type: Liberty seated: with motto over the eage.

(The mint marks are on the Rev., under the eagle)

Date	Amount Minted	Value	Date	Amount Minted	Value
1866	49,600	90.00	1871	1 million	40.00
1867	60,300	90.00	1871-CC	1,400	900.00
1868	182,700	75.00	1872	1 million	40.00
1869	424,300	40.00	1872-S	9,000	75.00
1870	433,000	40.00	1872-CC	3,100	400.00
1870-S	Unknown	Rare	1873	293,600	40.00
1870-CC	12,500	90.00	1873-CC	2,300	1000.00

Type: Liberty Head.

(The mint marks are on the Rev., under the eagle)

Date	Amount Minted	Very Fine	Unc	Date	Amount Minted	Very Fine	Unc
1878	10½ million	5.50	20.00	1882-CC	1¼ million	15.00	35.00
1878-S	9¾ million	5.50	15.00	1883	12¼ million	5.00	11.00
1878-CC	2¼ million	10.00	40.00	1883-O	8¾ million	5.00	10.00
1879	14¾ million	5.00	14.00	1883-S	6¼ million	9.00	200.00
1879-O	3 million	5.00	22.00	1883-CC	1¼ million	15.00	35.00
1879-S	9 million	5.00	11.00	1884	14 million	5.00	11.00
1879-CC	756,000	18.00	650.00	1884-O	9¾ million	5.00	9.00
1880	12⅔ million	5.00	11.00	1884-S	3⅓ million	7.00	1,100.00
1880-O	5⅓ million	5.00	20.00	1884-CC	1¼ million	15.00	35.00
1880-S	9 million	5.00	11.00	1885	17¾ million	5.00	9.00
1880-CC	591,000	18.00	80.00	1885-O	9¼ million	5.00	9.00
1881	9¼ million	5.00	14.00	1885-S	1½ million	9.00	40.00
1881-O	5¾ million	5.00	10.00	1885-CC	228,000	90.00	125.00
1881-S	12¾ million	5.00	11.00	1886	20 million	5.00	8.00
1881-CC	296,000	35.00	85.00	1886-O	10¾ million	6.00	125.00
1882	11 million	5.00	11.00	1886-S	750,000	9.00	50.00
1882-O	6 million	5.00	10.00	1887	20¼ million	5.00	9.00
1882-S	9¼ million	5.00	12.00	1887-O	11½ million	5.00	20.00

Date	Amount Minted	Very Fine	Unc	Date	Amount Minted	Very Fine	Unc
1887-S	1¾ million	7.00	25.00	1896	10 million	5.00	9.00
1888	19¼ million	5.00	9.00	1896-O	5 million	7.00	450.00
1888-O	12¼ million	5.00	15.00	1896-S	5 million	18.00	200.00
1888-S	657,000	11.50	50.00	1897	2¾ million	5.00	9.00
1889	21¾ million	5.00	9.00	1897-O	4 million	5.00	240.00
1889-O	11¾ million	5.00	35.00	1897-S	5¾ million	11.00	20.00
1889-S	700,000	11.00	45.00	1898	5¾ million	5.00	9.00
1889-CC	350,000	100.00	3,750.00	1898-O	4½ million	5.00	9.00
1890	16¾ million	5.00	10.00	1898-S	4 million	5.00	75.00
1890-O	10¾ million	5.00	15.00	1899	331,000	15.00	40.00
1890-S	8¼ million	5.00	20.00	1899-O	12¼ million	5.00	10.00
1890-CC	2⅓ million	12.00	120.00	1899-S	2½ million	11.00	70.00
1891	8¾ million	5.00	15.00	1900	8¾ million	5.00	9.00
1891-O	8 million	5.00	20.00	1900-O	12½ million	5.00	10.00
1891-S	5¼ million	5.00	20.00	1900-S	3½ million	10.00	50.00
1891-CC	1⅔ million	15.00	80.00	1901	7 million	13.00	500.00
1892	1 million	7.00	45.00	1901-O	13⅓ million	5.00	10.00
1892-O	2¾ million	7.00	45.00	1901-S	2¼ million	12.00	135.00
1892-S	1¼ million	12.00	4,250.00	1902	8 million	6.00	20.00
1892-CC	1⅓ million	20.00	200.00	1902-O	8⅔ million	5.00	9.00
1893	379,000	25.00	150.00	1902-S	1 ½ million	25.00	80.00
1893-O	300,000	35.00	700.00	1903	4⅔ million	7.00	18.00
1893-S	100,000	500.00	13,000.00	1903-O	4½ million	65.00	100.00
1893-CC	677,000	50.00	700.00	1903-S	1¼ million	25.00	90.00
1894	111,000	125.00	500.00	1904	2¾ million	5.00	30.00
1894-O	1¾ million	10.00	300.00	1904-O	3¾ million	5.00	9.00
1894-S	1¼ million	17.00	200.00	1904-S	2⅓ million	20.00	500.00
1895	880 proofs		10,000.00	1921	44⅔ million	5.00	6.00
1895-O	450,000	40.00	4,200.00	1921-D	20⅓ million	5.00	14.00
1895-S	400,000	70.00	500.00	1921-S	21⅔ million	5.00	14.00

Type: The Peace Dollar

(The mint marks are on the bottom of the Rev., to left of the eagle's wing)

Date	Amount Minted	Very Fine	Unc	Date	Amount Minted	Very Fine	Unc
1921	1 million	14.00	75.00	1926-D	2⅓ million	6.00	12.00
1922	51¾ million	5.00	6.00	1926-S	7 million	6.00	15.00
1922-D	15 million	5.00	10.00	1927	848,000	8.00	28.00
1922-S	17½ million	5.00	11.00	1927-D	1¼ million	7.00	70.00
1923	30¾ million	5.00	6.00	1927-S	866,000	7.00	45.00
1923-D	6¾ million	5.00	15.00	1928	361,000	55.00	100.00
1923-S	19 million	5.00	12.00	1928-S	1⅔ million	6.00	45.00
1924	11¾ million	5.00	7.00	1934	954,000	8.00	40.00
1924-S	1¾ million	7.00	55.00	1934-D	1½ million	7.00	45.00
1925	10¼ million	5.00	7.00	1934-S	1 million	20.00	700.00
1925-S	1⅔ million	7.00	30.00	1935	1½ million	7.00	24.00
1926	2 million	5.00	12.00	1935-S	2 million	6.00	60.00

Reg. Obv.
1971–1974

Reg. Rev.
1971–1974

Bicentennial
Obv.—1976

Bicentennial
Rev.—1976

Type: The Eisenhower Dollar

(The mint marks are on the obverse, below Eisenhower's neck)
(The valuations are for uncirculated coins)

Date/Type	Amount Minted	Value	Date/Type	Amount Minted	Value
1971 cupro-nickel,	47¾ million	1.50	1974-S cupro-nickel,	2⅔ million	2.50
1971-D cupro-nickel,	68½ million	1.25	1974-S silver,	2 million	2.50
1971-S silver,	6¾ million	2.00	1974-S silver, proof,	1⅓ million	3.50
1971-S silver, proof,	4¼ million	2.25	1975	none minted	
1972 cupro-nickel,	75¾ million	1.05	1976		1.10
1972-D cupro-nickel,	92½ million	1.05	1976-D		1.10
1972-S silver,	2¼ million	2.00	1976-S cupro-nickel, proof,		2.00
1972-S silver, proof,	2 million	2.25	1976-S silver,		3.50
1973 cupro-nickel,	2 million	2.00	1976-S silver, proof,		4.00
1973-D cupro-nickel,	2 million	2.00	1977 cupro-nickel,	12½ million	1.05
1973-S cupro-nickel, proof,	2¾ million	2.00	1977-D cupro-nickel,	33 million	1.05
1973-S silver,	1¾ million	3.50	1977-S cupro-nickel, proof,	3¼ million	2.00
1973-S silver, proof,	1 million	14.00	1978 cupro-nickel,	25¾ million	1.05
1974 cupro-nickel,	27⅓ million	1.05	1978-D cupro-nickel,	23 million	1.05
1974-D cupro-nickel,	45½ million	1.05	1978-S cupro-nickel, proof,	3 million	2.25

Type: The Anthony Dollar

(The mint marks are on the Obv., to the left of Anthony's neck)
(The valuations are for Uncirculated coins)
Type I—Mint mark is not distinct. Type II—Mint mark is clear.

Date	Amount Minted	Value	Date	Amount Minted	Value
1979-P	360¼ million	1.00	1980-S	20½ million	1.00
1979-D	288 million	1.00	1980-S	3½ million proofs	3.00
1979-S	109½ million	1.10	1981-P	3 million	1.50
1979-S Ty. I	3½ million proofs	3.00	1981-D	3¼ million	1.50
1979-S Ty. II	proof	30.00	1981-S	3½ million	1.50
1980-P	27½ million	1.00	1981-S Ty. I	4 million proofs	3.00
1980-D	41 ½ million	1.00	1981-S Ty. II	proof	50.00

Type: The Trade Dollar

(The mint marks are on the Rev., under the eagle)

Date	Amount Minted	Value	Date	Amount Minted	Value
1873	397,500	30.00	1877-S	9½ million	30.00
1873-S	703,000	50.00	1877-CC	534,000	50.00
1873-CC	124,500	60.00	1878	900 proofs	750.00
1874	987,800	30.00	1878-S	4¼ million	24.00
1874-S	2½ million	30.00	1878-CC	97,000	70.00
1874-CC	1⅓ million	30.00	1879	1,500 proofs	750.00
1875	218,900	100.00	1880	2,000 proofs	750.00
1875-S	4½ million	24.00	1881	1,000 proofs	750.00
1875-CC	1½ million	30.00	1882	1,100 proofs	750.00
1876	456,100	27.50	1883	1,000 proofs	750.00
1876-S	5¼ million	30.00	1884	10 proofs	—
1876-CC	509,000	40.00	1885	5 proofs	—
1877	3 million	24.00			

U.S. Silver Commemorative Coins

(All are Half Dollars of standard size and weight except the Isabella Quarter
of 1893, the Lafayette Dollar of 1900, the Olympic coins of 1984, the
Immigrant Half Dollar of 1986, and the Ellis Island Dollar.)

IMPORTANT NOTE: The valuations below are for coins in bright, new, uncirculated
condition. Pieces in used or circulated condition are worth less. The amount of coins
minted or in existence is shown to the left of the valuation. Because of speculation, the
valuations are subject to fluctuation. Coins in exceptionally choice condition are worth
considerably more than the prices listed.

COLUMBIAN, 1892–1893

For the World's Columbian Exposition of Chicago, where it was issued
on the 400th year of the discovery of
America. *Head of Columbus. Rev.
His flagship, the Santa Maria, over
global hemispheres.*

Date	Amount Minted	Value
1892	950,000 (used 4.50)	**20.00**
1893	1½ million (used 4.50)	**17.50**

ISABELLA QUARTER, 1893

For the same event as the Columbian Half Dollar. *Crowned head of
Queen Isabella of Spain. Rev. Female
spinner kneeling.*

Date	Amount Minted	Value
1893	24,191	**200.00**

LAFAYETTE DOLLAR, 1900

On the gift by the youth of
America to France of an
equestrian statue of Lafayette. *Conjoined heads of
Washington and Lafayette.
Rev. The statue as erected
in Paris*

Date	Amount Minted	Value
1900	36,026	**400.00**

PANAMA-PACIFIC, 1915

For the Panama-Pacific Exposition in
San Francisco on the opening of the
Panama Canal. *Columbia and child
standing at the Golden Gate. Rev.
Eagle and shield.*

Date	Amount Minted	Value
1915-S	27,134	**200.00**

ILLINOIS, 1918

On the 100th year of Illinois state-hood. *Head of Lincoln. Rev. Eagle standing to left.*

Date	Amount Minted	Value
1918	100,058	**45.00**

MAINE, 1920

On the 100th year of Maine state-hood. *The coat-of-arms of Maine. Rev. Wreath formed of pines and cones.*

Date	Amount Minted	Value
1920	50,028	**50.00**

PILGRIM, 1920–1921

On the 300th year of the Landing of the Pilgrims at Plymouth Rock. *Governor Bradford in Pilgrim dress. Rev. The ship Mayflower.*

Date	Amount Minted	Value
1920	152,000	**40.00**
1921	20,053	**50.00**

MISSOURI, 1921

On the 100th year of Missouri state-hood. *Bust of a Missouri pioneer. Rev. Pioneer and Indian standing. The "2 × 4" is located in front of the bust.*

Date	Amount Minted	Value
1921	15,400	**200.00**
1921 2 × 4	5,000	**225.00**

ALABAMA, 1921

On the 100th year of Alabama state-hood. *Conjoined heads of Gov. Bibb (1821) and Gov. Kilby (1921). Rev. Eagle. The "2 × 2" is located in the back of the busts.*

Date	Amount Minted	Value
1921	49,000	**100.00**
1921 2 × 2	5,000	**140.00**

GRANT, 1922
On the 100th year of his birth. *Uniformed bust of the General. Rev. A log cabin in the woods.* The * is located on the obverse, over the word, "Grant." Beware of added star.

Date	Amount Minted	Value
1922	67,200	**40.00**
1922*	4,250	**400.00**

MONROE DOCTRINE, 1923
On the 100th year of Monroe's famous Doctrine. *Conjoined heads of Monroe and John Q. Adams. Rev. Allegories depicting North and South America.*

Date	Amount Minted	Value
1923-S	274,077	**25.00**

HUGUENOT-WALLOON, 1924
On the 300th year of the settlement of New Netherlands by the Dutch. *Conjoined heads of Admiral Coligny and William the Silent. Rev. The ship New Netherlands.*

Date	Amount Minted	Value
1924	142,080	**40.00**

LEXINGTON-CONCORD, 1925
On the 150th year of these famous battles of 1775. *Armed Minute Man standing. Rev. View of Old Belfry.*

Date	Amount Minted	Value
1925	162,099	**35.00**

STONE MOUNTAIN, 1925
On the erection of a Memorial on Stone Mountain to the valor of the Soldier of the South. *Gen. "Stonewall" Jackson and Gen. Robert E. Lee on horseback. Rev. Eagle on mountain peak.*

Date	Amount Minted	Value
1925	1⅓ million (used 9.00)	**22.00**

CALIFORNIA JUBILEE, 1925
On the 75th year of California State-hood. A "forty-niner" panning gold. Rev. Grizzly bear.

Date	Amount Minted	Value
1925-S	86,500	**50.00**

FORT VANCOUVER, 1925
On the 100th year of the erection of Fort Vancouver. Head of Dr. John McLaughlin, who built the Fort. Rev. Armed pioneer standing before mountian.

Date	Amount Minted	Value
1925	14,994	**150.00**

U.S. INDEPENDENCE, 1926
On the 150th year of the Declaration of Independence. Conjoined heads of Washington and Coolidge. Rev. The Liberty Bell.

Date	Amount Minted	Value
1926	141,120	**30.00**

OREGON TRAIL, 1926–1939
In commemoration of this popular but perilous highway to the west. Indian Chief standing before a map of the U.S. Rev. The famous covered wagon of the Trail.

Date	Amount Minted	Value
1926	48,030	**50.00**
1926-S	86,354	**50.00**
1928	6,028	**100.00**
1933-D	5,008	**150.00**
1934-D	7,006	**75.00**
1936	10,006	**60.00**
1936-S	5,006	**85.00**
1937-D	12,008	**70.00**
1938-P-D-S	6,005 sets, set of 3	**400.00**
1939-P-D-S	3,004 sets, set of 3	**650.00**

VERMONT, 1927
On the 150th year both of the Battle of Bennington and of Vermont's in-dependence. Head of Ira Allen. Rev. Vermont mountain lion.

Date	Amount Minted	Value
1927	28,142	**80.00**

HAWAII, 1928
On the 150th year of Captain Cook's discovery of the Hawaiian Islands. *Bust of the Captain. Rev. Hawaiian Chief in native dress.*

Date	Amount Minted	Value
1928	10,008	**550.00**

MARYLAND, 1934
On the 300th year of the founding of the Colony. *Head of Lord Baltimore, the founder. Rev. The coat-of-arms of Maryland.*

Date	Amount Minted	Value
1934	25,015	**75.00**

BOONE, 1934–1938
On the 200th year of the birth of Daniel Boone. *Head of Boone. Rev. Standing figures of Boone and Indian Chief, Black Fish.*

Date	Amount Minted	Value
1934	10,007	**45.00**
1935	10,010, Set of 3	**125.00**
1935-D-S	5,005 per Mint	

The following have the date "1934" on the reverse above "Pioneer Year."

Date	Amount Minted	Value
1935	10,008, Set of 3	**300.00**
1935-P-D-S	2,003 per Mint	
1936	12,012, Set of 3	
1936-P-D-S	5,006 per Mint	**125.00**
1937	9,810, Set of 3	
1937-P-D-S	2,506 per Mint	**375.00**
1938-P-D-S	2,100 Set of 3	**450.00**
Type coin (any date)		**45.00**

TEXAS, 1934–1938

On the 100th year of the Independence of Texas. *Eagle on a "lone star." Rev. Winged Victory between heads of Sam Houston and Stephen Austin.*

Date	Amount Minted	Value
1934	61,350	**50.00**
1935	9,934	**50.00**
1935-D	10,007	**60.00**
1935-S	10,008	**60.00**
1936	8,911	**60.00**
1936-D	9,039	**60.00**
1936-S	9,064	**60.00**
1937-P-D-S	6,571 sets, set of 3	**160.00**
1938-P-D-S	3,775 sets, set of 3	**300.00**

ARKANSAS, 1935–1939

On the 100th year of Arkansas Statehood. *Liberty head and Indian head conjoined. Rev. Eagle.*

Date	Amount Minted	Value
1935	13,012	**45.00**
1935-D-S	5,505 pair, set of 2	**120.00**
1936-P-D-S	9,660 sets, set of 3	**125.00**
1937-P-D-S	5,505 sets, set of 3	**130.00**
1938-P-D-S	3,1 55 sets, set of 3	**200.00**
1939-P-D-S	2,104 sets, set of 3	**400.00**

CONNECTICUT, 1935

On the 300th year of the founding of the Colony. *The famous Charter Oak Tree. Rev. Eagle.*

Date	Amount Minted	Value
1935	25,018	**90.00**

HUDSON, 1935

On the 150th year of the founding of the city of Hudson, N.Y. *Hudson's ship, the Half Moon. Rev. Neptune on whale, a mermaid in the background.*

Date	Amount Minted	Value
1935	10,008	**260.00**

SAN DIEGO, 1935–1936

For the California-Pacific International Exposition in San Diego. *Seated female and bear. View of Exposition buildings.*

Date	Amount Minted	Value
1935-S	70,132	**30.00**
1936-D	30,092	**40.00**

OLD SPANISH TRAIL, 1935

On the 400th year of the de Vaca Expedition across the land area of the Gulf of Mexico. *Skull of a cow. Rev. Yucca tree and map of the Trail.*

Date	Amount Minted	Value
1935	10,008	**475.00**

ALBANY, 1936

On the 250th year of Albany's City Charter. *Beaver gnawing on maple twigs. Rev. Standing figures of Gov. Dongan, Peter Schuyler and Robert Livingston.*

Date	Amount Minted	Value
1936	16,887	**125.00**

BRIDGEPORT, 1936

On the 100th year of Bridgeport, Conn. as a city. *Head of P. T. Barnum. Rev. Modern style eagle.*

Date	Amount Minted	Value
1936	25,015	**65.00**

CINCINNATI, 1936

On the 50th year of Cincinnati as a music center. *Head of Stephen Foster. Rev. Girl playing harp.*

Date	Amount Minted	Value
1936	5,005	**125.00**
1936-D	5,005	**125.00**
1936-S	5,006	**125.00**

COLUMBIA, S.C., 1936

On the 150th year of the founding of the city. *Standing figure of Justice between the Capitol buildings of 1786 and 1936. Rev. Palmetto tree.*

Date	Amount Minted	Value
1936	9,007	**110.00**
1936-D	8,009	**110.00**
1936-S	8,007	**110.00**

DELAWARE, 1936

On the 300th year of the Swedish landing in Wilmington. *The Swedish ship Kalmar Nyckel. Rev. Old Swede's Church in Wilmington.*

Date	Amount Minted	Value
1936	25,015	**125.00**

ELGIN, ILLINOIS, 1936

On the 100th year of the founding of the city. *Bearded head of a pioneer. Rev. Four pioneers standing.*

Date	Amount Minted	Value
1936	25,015	**110.00**

GETTYSBURG, 1936

For the 75th Anniversary of the Battle of Gettysburg, 1863–1938. *Conjoined heads of a Union and Confederate soldier. Rev. Union and Confederate shields.*

Date	Amount Minted	Value
1936	26,928	**130.00**

GREAT LAKES, 1936

For the Great Lakes Exposition on the 100th year of Cleveland, Ohio. *Head of Moses Cleaveland. Rev. Map of the Great Lakes.*

Date	Amount Minted	Value
1936	50,030	**30.00**

LONG ISLAND, 1936

On the 300th year of the landing at Jamaica Bay, Long Island by Dutch Settlers. *Conjoined heads of a Dutchman and Indian. Rev. Sailing ship.*

Date	Amount Minted	Value
1936	81,773	**35.00**

LYNCHBURG, 1936

On the 150th year of the city charter given to Lynchburg, Virginia. *Head of Senator Carter Glass. Rev. Liberty standing at old courthouse.*

Date	Amount Minted	Value
1936	20,013	**85.00**

NORFOLK, 1936

On the 200th year of Norfolk, Virginia, becoming a royal borough. *Sailing ship as on the city shield. Rev. A large mace.*

Date	Amount Minted	Value
1936	15,000	**275.00**

RHODE ISLAND, 1936

On the 300th year of the founding of Providence by Roger Williams. *Roger Williams in canoe being welcomed by Indian. Rev. Large anchor.*

Date	Amount Minted	Value
1936	20,013	**40.00**
1936-D	15,010	**40.00**
1936-S	15,011	**40.00**

ROBINSON, 1936

On the 100th year of Arkansas statehood. *Head of Senator Joseph T. Robinson. Rev. Eagle. (Identical to the reverse of the Arkansas issues of 1935–1939; the only instance of the same event being commemorated by two different types of Half Dollars.)*

Date	Amount Minted	Value
1936	25,265	**40.00**

SAN FRANCISCO, 1936

On the opening of the San Fran-cisco-Oakland Bay Bridge. *California grizzly bear. Rev. View of the bridge.*

Date	Amount Minted	Value
1936-S	71,369	**60.00**

WISCONSIN, 1936

On the 100th year of the formation of Wisconsin Territory. *Forearm holding pickaxe over ore. Rev. Badger on log.*

Date	Amount Minted	Value
1936	25,015	**90.00**

YORK COUNTY, ME., 1936

On the 300th year of the founding of York County, Maine. *Brown's Garrison at Saco. Rev. The seal of the County.*

Date	Amount Minted	Value
1936	25,015	**100.00**

ANTIETAM, 1937

On the 75th year of the Battle of An-tietam. *Conjoined heads of the Union's Gen. McClellan and the Con-federacy's Gen. Lee. Rev. Burnside Bridge for which the battle was fought.*

Date	Amount Minted	Value
1937	18,028	**250.00**

ROANOKE, 1937

On the 350th year of the colonization of Roanoke Island by Sir Walter Ra-leigh; also on the birth of Virginia Dare in 1587, the first white child born in America. *Bust of Sir Walter Raleigh. Rev. Mother holding Virginia Dare.*

Date	Amount Minted	Value
1937	29,030	**115.00**

NEW ROCHELLE, 1938
On the 250th year of the founding of New Rochelle, New York, by the Huguenots. *Lord Pell holding fatted calf. Rev. Fleur-de-lis.*

Date	Amount Minted	Value
1938	15,266	**185.00**

IOWA, 1946
On the 100th year of Iowa Statehood. *Eagle on scroll, Rev. The old Capitol Statehouse at Iowa City.*

Date	Amount Minted	Value
1946	100,057	**40.00**

B.T.W., 1946–1951
In honor of this great black leader and educator. *Head of Booker T. Washington. Rev. View of the log cabin of his birth and of the Hall of Fame where he is inscribed.*

Date	Amount Minted	Value
1946	1 million	**5.00**
1946-D	200,113	**8.00**
1946-S	500,279	**7.00**
1947-P-D-S	100,017 sets, set of 3	**25.00**
1948-P-D-S	8,005 sets, set of 3	**50.00**
1949-P-D-S	6,004 sets, set of 3	**100.00**
1950-P-D-S	6,004 sets, set of 3	**50.00**
1950-S	403,996	**8.00**
1951	503,078	**8.00**
1951-P-D-S	7,004 sets, set of 3	**50.00**

G.W.C.-B.T.W., 1951–1954
In honor of the famous black leaders, George Washington Carver and Booker T. Washington. *Their conjoined heads. Rev. Map of the United States.*

Date	Amount Minted	Value
1951	100,014	**7.00**
1951-P-D-S	10,004 sets, set of 3	**30.00**
1952	2 million	**7.00**
1952-P-D-S	8,000 sets, set of 3	**30.00**
1953-P-D-S	8,000 sets, set of 3	**40.00**
1953-S	100,000	**9.00**
1954-P-D-S	12,000 sets, set of 3	**30.00**
1954-S	110,000	**9.00**

GEORGE WASHINGTON, 1982

On the 250th Anniversary of the birth of the first President. *Washington on horseback. Rev. View of Mount Vernon.*

Date	Amount Minted	Value
1982-D Uncirculated	2,210,458	**2.50**
1982-S Proof	4,894,004	**2.50**

LOS ANGELES OLYMPIC GAMES, 1983–1984

Issued to help raise funds for the staging of the 1984 Summer Olympic Games in Los Angeles. *Both issues bear an eagle on the obverse, with the reverse of the 1983 coin depicting a discus thrower and the 1984 coin the gateway to the Los Angeles Coliseum.*

Denom	Year	Amount Minted	Value
1 Dollar	1983-P Unc.	920,485	**5.00**
1 Dollar	1983-D Unc.	597,157	**13.00**
1 Dollar	1983-S Unc.	662,837	**11.00**
1 Dollar	1983-S Proof	4,575,603	**5.00**
1 Dollar	1984-P Unc.	470,131	**7.00**
1 Dollar	1984-D Unc.	316,778	**22.00**
1 Dollar	1984-S Unc.	339,970	**25.00**
1 Dollar	1984-S Proof	2,623,609	**6.00**

IMMIGRANT, 1986

On the centennial of the Statue of Liberty. Commemorates the immigrants who passed through Ellis Island before entering New York. *Rising sun behind statue. Rev. Immigrant Family on Ellis Island.*

Denom	Year	Amount Minted	Value
Half Dollar	1986-D Unc.	928,008	**1.50**
Half Dollar	1986-S Proof	6,925,627	**1.50**

ELLIS ISLAND, 1986

On the centennial of the Statue of Liberty. Commemorates Ellis Island the "Gateway to America." *Statue in front of the Ellis Island immigration facility. Rev. Liberty's hand holding torch.*

Denom	Year	Amount Minted	Value
1 Dollar	1986-D Unc.	723,635	**4.50**
1 Dollar	1986-S Proof	6,414,638	**4.50**

Coins shown at approximately ⁴/₅ actual size.

Coins shown at approximately ⁴/₅ actual size.

CONSTITUTION BICENTENNIAL, 1987

On the 200th anniversary of the Constitution of the United States. *Quill pen superimposed over a copy of the Constitution. Rev. A group of American men and women from the past two centuries.*

Denomination	Year	Amount Minted	Value
1 Dollar	1987-P Unc.	451,629	**5.00**
1 Dollar	1987-S Proof	2,747,116	**5.00**

Coins shown at approximately 85% of actual size.

1988 OLYMPICS

To raise money for the 1988 American Olympic Teams.

Denomination	Year	Amount Minted	Value
1 Dollar	1988-D Unc.	191,368	**10.00**
1 Dollar	1988-S Proof	1,354,366	**4.00**

CONGRESS BICENTENNIAL, 1989

On the 200th Anniversary of the United States Congress. *The obverse portrays a symbolic bust of Freedom; Rev. The Congress.*

Denomination	Type	Year	Amount Minted	Value
Half Dollar	Copper-Nickel, Uncirculated	1989-D	163,753	7.00
Half Dollar	Copper-Nickel, Proof	1989-S	767,897, Proof	3.00
1 Dollar	Silver, Uncirculated	1989-D	135,203	12.50
1 Dollar	Silver, Proof	1989-S	762,198, Proof	7.50

EISENHOWER CENTENNIAL, 1990

On the 100th Anniversary of Eisenhower's birth. *The conjoined heads of Eisenhower as President facing right, and as General facing left. Rev. Eisenhower's home.*

Denomination	Type	Year	Amount Minted	Value
1 Dollar	Silver, Uncirculated	1990-W	241,669	12.00
1 Dollar	Silver, Proof	1990-P	1,144,461	8.00

MOUNT RUSHMORE ANNIVERSARY, 1991

On the 50th anniversary of the historic landmark. Rev. A Buffalo.

Denomination	Type	Year	Amount Minted	Value
Half Dollar	Copper-Nickel, Uncirculated	1991-D	172,754	6.00
Half Dollar	Copper-Nickel, Proof	1991-S	753,257	6.50
1 Dollar	Silver, Uncirculated	1991-P	133,138	20.00
1 Dollar	Silver, Proof	1991-S	738,419	17.50

KOREAN WAR MEMORIAL, 1991

On the 38th Anniversary of the end of the historic conflict. Rev. A map of Korea; an eagle.

Denomination	Type	Year	Amount Minted	Value
1 Dollar	Silver, Uncirculated	1991-D	213,409	8.00
1 Dollar	Silver, Proof	1991-P	618,488	7.50

UNITED SERVICE ORGANIZATIONS, 1991

To honor the 50th Anniversary, founded to aid the Armed Services personnel.

Denomination	Type	Year	Amount Minted	Value
1 Dollar	Silver, Uncirculated	1991-D	124,958	**20.00**
1 Dollar	Silver, Proof	1991-S	321,275	**16.00**

1992 OLYMPICS

To raise money for the 1992 American Olympic Team

Denomination	Type	Year	Amount Minted	Value
Half Dollar	Copper-Nickel	1992-P	161,619	**3.00**
Half Dollar	Copper-Nickel	1992-S	519,699	**4.50**
One Dollar	Silver	1992-D	187,562	**16.00**
One Dollar	Silver	1992-S	504,544	**18.00**

COLUMBUS QUINCENTENARY, 1992

On the 500th Anniversary of Christopher Columbus' voyage.

Denomination	Type	Year	Amount Minted	Value
Half Dollar	Copper-Nickel, Uncirculated	1992-D	135,718	**6.00**
Half Dollar	Copper-Nickel, Proof	1992-S	390,255	**6.00**
1 Dollar	Silver, Uncirculated	1992-D	106,962	**15.00**
1 Dollar	Silver, Proof	1992-P	385,290	**12.00**

WHITE HOUSE BICENTENNIAL, 1992

On the 200th Anniversary of the White House. This coin is the first Proof commemorative with the "W" (West Point) mint mark. Rev.; James Hoban, the original architect.

Denomination	Type	Year	Amount Minted	Value
1 Dollar	Silver, Uncirculated	1992-D	123,803	**30.00**
1 Dollar	Silver, Proof	1992-W	375,849	**30.00**

BILL OF RIGHTS, 1993

Denomination	Type	Year	Amount Minted	Value
Half Dollar	Silver, Uncirculated	1993-W	173,224	5.00
Half Dollar	Silver, Proof	1993-S	559,758	4.50
1 Dollar	Silver, Uncirculated	1993-D	92,415	12.00
1 Dollar	Silver, Proof	1993-S	515,038	9.00

WORLD WAR II, 1993

On the 50th Anniversary of World War.

Denomination	Type	Year	Amount Minted	Value
Half Dollar	Copper-Nickel, Uncirculated	1993-P	192,968	5.00
Half Dollar	Copper-Nickel, Proof	1993-P	290,343	4.00
1 Dollar	Silver, Uncirculated	1993-D	94,700	16.00
1 Dollar	Silver, Proof	1993-W	322,422	17.50

WOMEN IN THE MILITARY, 1994

Honoring all United States women veterans.

Denomination	Type	Year	Amount Minted	Value
1 Dollar	Silver, Uncirculated	1994-W		30.00
1 Dollar	Silver, Proof	1994-P		30.00

WORLD CUP SOCCER, 1993

Commemorating the United States hosting of the tournament.

Denomination	Type	Year	Amount Minted	Value
Half Dollar	Copper-Nickel, Uncirculated	1994-D		**5.00**
Half Dollar	Copper-Nickel, Proof	1994-P		**6.00**
1 Dollar	Silver, Uncirculated	1994-D		**15.00**
1 Dollar	Silver, Proof	1994-S		**30.00**

THOMAS JEFFERSON, 1994

Commemorating the 250th Anniversary of his birth.

Denomination	Type	Year	Amount Minted	Value
1 Dollar	Silver, Uncirculated	1994-P		**30.00**
1 Dollar	Silver, Proof	1994-S		**30.00**

VIETNAM WAR MEMORIAL, 1994

On the 10th Anniversary of the Memorial in Washington, D.C.

Denomination	Type	Year	Amount Minted	Value
1 Dollar	Silver, Uncirculated	1994-W		**30.00**
1 Dollar	Silver, Proof	1994-S		**30.00**

PRISONERS OF WAR, 1994

Honoring the United States prisoners of war.

Denomination	Type	Year	Amount Minted	Value
1 Dollar	Silver, Uncirculated	1994-W		**30.00**
1 Dollar	Silver, Proof	1994-P		**30.00**

U.S. Gold Commemorative Coins

IMPORTANT NOTE: The valuations below are for coins in bright, new, uncirculated condition. Pieces in used or circulated condition are worth less. The amount of coins minted or in existence is shown to the left of the valuation.

LOUISIANA PURCHASE ISSUE, 1903

Two types of Gold Dollars were struck to commemorate the Centennial of the Louisiana Purchase. *The same reverse appears on both.*

Denomination	Year	Description	Amount Minted	Value
1 Dollar	1903	Head of Jefferson	17,375	**250.00**
1 Dollar	1903	Head of McKinley	17,375	**245.00**

LEWIS AND CLARK ISSUE, 1904–1905

Two dates of a Gold Dollar were struck to commemorate the Centennial of the Lewis and Clark Expedition. *The head of Lewis appears on one side and that of Clark on the other.*

Denomination	Year	Amount Minted	Value
1 Dollar	1904	9,997	**500.00**
1 Dollar	1905	10,000	**550.00**

PANAMA PACIFIC ISSUE, 1915

Four types of gold coins were struck for the Panama-Pacific Exposition commemorating the opening of the Panama Canal.

Denomination	Year	Description	Amount Minted	Value
1 Dollar	1915-S	Head of worker	25,000	**275.00**

Denomination	Year	Description	Amount Minted	Value
2½ Dollars	1915-S	Columbia on hippocampus	6,749	**925.00**

Denomination	Year	Description	Amount Minted	Value
50 Dollars	1915-S, round	Head of Minerva	483	**16,000.00**
50 Dollars	1915-S, octagonal	Head of Minerva	645	**14,500.00**

MCKINLEY MEMORIAL ISSUE, 1916-1917

Two dates of a Gold Dollar were struck to commemorate the erection of the McKinley Memorial at Niles, Ohio. *The obverse shows his head, and the reverse the memorial building.*

Denomination	Year	Amount Minted	Value
1 Dollar	1916	9,977	**250.00**
1 Dollar	1917	10,000	**275.00**

GRANT CENTENNIAL ISSUE, 1922

Two varieties of a Gold Dollar were struck to commemorate the 100th year of Grant's birth. *His head appears on the obverse and a log cabin on the reverse. The star is located on the obverse, over the word, "Grant."*

Denomination	Year	Amount Minted	Value
1 Dollar	1922	5,000	**900.00**
1 Dollar	1922 with star	5,000	**1,000.00**

U.S. INDEPENDENCE ISSUE, 1926

A 2¹/₂ Dollar gold piece was struck to commemorate the Sesquicentennial (150th year) of the Declaration of Independence. *The obverse shows Liberty standing; the reverse a view of Independence Hall in Philadelphia.*

Denomination	Year	Amount Minted	Value
2¹/₂ Dollar	1926	46,019	**225.00**

LOS ANGELES OLYMPIC GAMES, 1984

To raise funds for the staging of the Games. *Struck at the West Point, NY Mint facility.*

Denomination	Year	Amount Minted	Value
10 Dollars	1984-W Unc.	100,000	**140.00**
10 Dollars	1984-W Proof	661,000	**140.00**
10 Dollars	1984-P Proof only	40,000	**175.00**
10 Dollars	1984-D Proof only	44,000	**150.00**
10 Dollars	1984-S Proof only	55,000	**140.00**

STATUE OF LIBERTY, 1986

On the centennial of the Statue of Liberty.
Head of statue. Rev. American eagle in flight.

Denomination	Year	Amount Minted	Value
5 Dollars	1986-W Unc.	500,000	**75.00**
5 Dollars	1986-W Proof	500,000	**75.00**

CONSTITUTION BICENTENNIAL, 1987

Coins shown at approximately 150% of actual size.

On the 200th anniversary of the U.S. Constitution.
Eagle holding quill pen. Rev. Quill pen under "We the People."

Denomination	Year	Amount Minted	Value
5 Dollars, Uncirculated	1987-W	214,225	**70.00**
5 Dollars, Proof	1987-W	651,659	**70.00**

1988 OLYMPICS

To raise money for the 1988 American Olympic Teams. *Head of Liberty. Rev. Flame.*

Denomination	Year	Amount Minted	Value
5 Dollars, Uncirculated	1988-W	62,913	**70.00**
5 Dollars, Proof	1988-W	281,465	**70.00**

CONGRESS BICENTENNIAL, 1989

On the 200th Anniversary of the Congress.
Obverse portrays the Capitol Dome. Rev. Eagle

Denomination	Year	Amount Minted	Value
5 Dollars, Uncirculated	1989-W	48,899	**70.00**
5 Dollars Proof	1989-W	164,690	**70.00**

MOUNT RUSHMORE, 1991

On the 50th anniversary of the historic landmark.

Denomination	Year	Amount Minted	Value
5 Dollars, Uncirculated	1991-W	31,959	**70.00**
5 Dollars, Proof	1991-W	111,991	**70.00**

1992 OLYMPICS

To raise money for the American teams.

Denomination	Year	Amount Minted	Value
5 Dollars, Uncirculated	1992-W	27,732	**85.00**
5 Dollars, Proof	1992-W	77,313	**85.00**

COLUMBUS QUINCENTENARY

On the 500th Anniversary of Christopher Columbus' voyage.

Denomination	Year	Amount Minted	Value
5 Dollars, Uncirculated	1992-W	24,331	**120.00**
5 Dollars, Proof	1992-W	79,734	**85.00**

BILL OF RIGHTS

Denomination	Year	Amount Minted	Value
5 Dollars, Uncirculated	1993-W	22,897	**110.00**
5 Dollars, Proof	1993-W	79,422	**115.00**

WORLD WAR II

On the 50th Anniversary of World War.

Denomination	Year	Amount Minted	Value
5 Dollars, Uncirculated	1993-W	23,089	**100.00**
5 Dollars, Proof	1993-W	65,462	**100.00**

WORLD CUP SOCCER

Commemorating the United States hosting of the tournament.

Denomination	Year	Amount Minted	Value
5 Dollars, Uncirculated	1994-W		**120.00**
5 Dollars, Proof	1994-W		**130.00**

United States Gold Coins

(The valuations are tor coins in choice VF-EF condition. Americans traveling abroad are cautioned to beware ot counterteit U.S. gold pieces in all denominations, which have been produced in many parts ot Europe and Asia.)

1 DOLLAR GOLD PIECES

Type: Liberty head with coronet. Small size.

(The mint marks are on the Rev., under the wreath)

Date	Amount Minted	Value	Date	Amount Minted	Value
1849	688,600	90.00	1852	2 million	90.00
1849-O	215,000	95.00	1852-O	140,000	95.00
1849-C	11,600	250.00	1852-C	9,400	200.00
1849-D	21,600	200.00	1852-D	6,400	350.00
1850	482,000	90.00	1853	4 million	90.00
1850-O	14,000	150.00	1853-O	290,000	100.00
1850-C	7,000	400.00	1853-C	11,500	300.00
1850-D	8,400	350.00	1853-D	6,600	450.00
1851	3¹⁄₃ million	90.00	1854	Part of 1²⁄₃ million	90.00
1851-O	290,000	100.00	1854-D	2,900	600.00
1851-C	41,300	240.00	1854-S	14,600	200.00
1851-D	9,900	225.00			

Type: Small Liberty head with feather head-dress. Large size.

(The mint marks are on the Rev., under the wreath)

Date	Amount Minted	Value	Date	Amount Minted	Value
1854	Part of 1²⁄₃ million	200.00	1855-C	9,800	650.00
1855	758,300	200.00	1855-D	1,800	1,750.00
1855-O	55,000	400.00	1856-S	24,600	450.00

(The valuations in this book are based on the coins being in G-VG condition, unless otherwise noted.)

Type: Large Liberty head with feather head-dress. Large size.

(The mint marks are on the Rev., under the wreath)

Date	Amount Minted	Value	Date	Amount Minted	Value
1856	1¾ million	95.00	1868	10,500	140.00
1856-D	1,500	2,500.00	1869	5,900	175.00
1857	774,800	80.00	1870	6,300	140.00
1857-C	13,300	400.00	1870-S	3,000	275.00
1857-D	3,500	600.00	1871	3,900	135.00
1857-S	10,000	300.00	1872	3,500	135.00
1858	118,000	80.00	1873	125,100	80.00
1858-D	3,500	450.00	1874	198,800	80.00
1858-S	10,000	300.00	1875	400	1,750.00
1859	168,200	80.00	1876	3,200	140.00
1859-C	5,200	300.00	1877	3,900	100.00
1859-D	5,000	500.00	1878	3,000	125.00
1859-S	15,000	200.00	1879	3,000	100.00
1860	36,700	80.00	1880	1,600	100.00
1860-D	1,600	1,400.00	1881	7,700	80.00
1860-S	13,000	175.00	1882	5,000	80.00
1861	527,500	80.00	1883	10,800	80.00
1861-D	Unknown	3,000.00	1884	6,200	80.00
1862	1⅓ million	80.00	1885	12,200	80.00
1863	6,200	275.00	1886	6,000	80.00
1864	5,900	200.00	1887	8,500	80.00
1865	3,700	200.00	1888	16,100	80.00
1866	7,200	200.00	1889	30,700	80.00
1867	5,200	240.00			

2½ DOLLAR GOLD PIECES (QUARTER EAGLES)

Type: Liberty head; without stars on Obv.

Date	Amount Minted	Value
1796	Part of 1,400	6,000.00

Type: Liberty head; with stars on Obv.

Date	Amount Minted	Value	Date	Amount Minted	Value
1796	Part of 1,400	6,000,00	1804	3,300	2,000.00
1797	1,700	5,000.00	1805	1,800	2,000.00
1798	600	2,000.00	1806	1,600	2,000.00
1802/over 1	2,600	2,000.00	1807	6,800	2,000.00

Type: Draped bust of Liberty with round cap.

Date	Amount Minted	Value
1808	2,700	**9,000.00**

Type: Undraped head of Liberty with round cap; with motto over eagle.

Date	Amount Minted	Value	Date	Amount Minted	Value
1821	6,400	**2,500.00**	1830	4,500	**2,250.00**
1824 over 21	2,600	**2,700.00**	1831	4,500	**2,250.00**
1825	4,400	**2,500.00**	1832	4,400	**2,250.00**
1826 over 25	800	**3,000.00**	1833	4,200	**2,250.00**
1827	2,800	**3,000.00**	1834	4,000	**7,500.00**
1829	3,400	**2,250.00**			

Type: Liberty head with ribbon; without motto over eagle.

(The mint marks are on the Obv., over the date)

Date	Amount Minted	Value	Date	Amount Minted	Value
1834	112,200	**150.00**	1838-C	7,900	**650.00**
1835	131,400	**150.00**	1839	27,000	**150.00**
1836	548,000	**150.00**	1839-O	17,800	**250.00**
1837	45,100	**150.00**	1839-C	18,200	**375.00**
1838	47,000	**150.00**	1839-D	13,700	**650.00**
			1839-O	17,800	**350.00**

Type: Liberty head with coronet.

(The mint marks are on the Rev., under the eagle. The "CAL" on the 1848 is over the eagle and represents gold mined in California)

Date	Amount Minted	Value	Date	Amount Minted	Value
1840	18,900	200.00	1854-O	153,000	100.00
1840-O	26,200	150.00	1854-C	7,300	350.00
1840-C	12,800	400.00	1854-D	1,800	1,400.00
1840-D	3,500	1,000.00	1854-S	246	30,000.00
1841	A few proofs	—	1855	235,500	90.00
1841-C	10,300	300.00	1855-C	3,700	750.00
1841-D	4,200	900.00	1855-D	1,100	2,200.00
1842	2,800	500.00	1856	384,200	100.00
1842-O	19,800	200.00	1856-O	21,100	140.00
1842-C	6,700	750.00	1856-C	7,900	200.00
1842-D	4,600	900.00	1856-D	874	1,500.00
1843	100,500	125.00	1856-S	71,100	100.00
1843-O	368,000	125.00	1857	214,100	90.00
1843-C	26,100	300.00	1857-O	34,000	100.00
1843-D	36,200	350.00	857-D	2,400	500.00
1844	6,800	200.00	1857-S	68,000	100.00
1844-C	11,600	350.00	1858	47,400	100.00
1844-D	17,300	350.00	1858-C	9,100	350.00
1845	91,100	150.00	1859	39,400	100.00
1845-O	4,000	250.00	1859-D	2,200	750.00
1845-D	19,500	350.00	1859-S	15,200	175.00
1846	21,600	200.00	1860	22,700	100.00
1846-O	66,000	175.00	1860-C	7,500	400.00
1846-C	4,800	600.00	1860-S	35,600	125.00
1846-D	19,300	450.00	1861	1¼ million	100.00
1847	29,800	175.00	1861-S	24,000	200.00
1847-O	124,000	150.00	1862	112,400	100.00
1847-C	23,200	375.00	1862-S	8,000	450.00
1847-D	15,800	325.00	1863	30 proofs	—
1848	7,500	300.00	1863-S	10,800	250.00
1848-CAL	1,400	5,000.00	1864	2,900	3,500.00
1848-C	16,800	450.00	1865	1,500	2,500.00
1848-D	13,800	350.00	1865-S	23,400	120.00
1849	23,300	225.00	1866	3,100	750.00
1849-C	10,220	300.00	1866-S	39,000	175.00
1849-D	10,900	400.00	1867	3,200	200.00
1850	252,900	100.00	1867-S	28,000	125.00
1850-O	84,000	120.00	1868	3,600	125.00
1850-C	9,100	250.00	1868-S	34,000	100.00
1850-D	12,100	350.00	1869	4,300	125.00
1851	1⅓ million	90.00	1869-S	29,500	100.00
1851-O	148,000	100.00	1870	4,600	125.00
1851-C	14,900	350.00	1870-S	16,000	100.00
1851-D	11,300	300.00	1871	5,300	150.00
1852	1¼ million	90.00	1871-S	22,000	100.00
1852-O	142,000	100.00	1872	3,000	225.00
1852-C	9,800	325.00	1872-S	18,000	120.00
1852-D	4,000	500.00	1873	178,000	90.00
1853	1⅓ million	90.00	1873-S	27,000	125.00
1853-D	3,200	800.00	1874	3,900	150.00
1854	596,300	90.00	1875	420	2,000.00

Date	Amount Minted	Value	Date	Amount Minted	Value
1875-S	11,600	100.00	1890	8,800	90.00
1876	4,200	150.00	1891	11,000	90.00
1876-S	5,000	140.00	1892	2,500	90.00
1877	1,700	200.00	1893	30,100	90.00
1877-S	35,400	90.00	1894	4,100	90.00
1878	286,300	90.00	1895	6,100	140.00
1878-S	178,000	90.00	1896	19,200	90.00
1879	89,000	90.00	1897	29,900	90.00
1879-S	43,500	120.00	1898	24,200	90.00
1880	3,000	120.00	1899	27,300	90.00
1881	680	750.00	1900	67,200	90.00
1882	4,000	120.00	1901	91,300	90.00
1883	2,000	125.00	1902	133,700	90.00
1884	2,000	125.00	1903	201,300	90.00
1885	887	300.00	1904	161,000	90.00
1886	4,100	125.00	1905	217,900	90.00
1887	6,300	100.00	1906	176,500	90.00
1888	16,100	90.00	1907	336,400	90.00
1889	17,600	90.00			

Type: Indian Head

(The mint marks are on the Rev., to the left of the value)

Date	Amount Minted	Value	Date	Amount Minted	Value
1908	565,000	90.00	1914-D	448,000	90.00
1909	441,900	90.00	1915	606,100	90.00
1910	492,700	90.00	1925-D	578,000	90.00
1911	704,200	90.00	1926	446,000	90.00
1911-D	55,700	700.00	1927	388,000	90.00
1912	616,200	90.00	1928	416,000	90.00
1913	722,200	90.00	192	32,200	90.00
1914	240,100	90.00			

3 DOLLAR GOLD PIECES

Type: Liberty head with feather head-dress

(The mint marks are on the Rev., under the wreath)

Date	Amount Minted	Value	Date	Amount Minted	Value
1854	138,600	325.00	1870	3,500	400.00
1854-O	24,000	400.00	1870-S	2	Very Rare
1854-D	1,100	5,000.00	1871	1,300	500.00
1855	50,600	375.00	1872	2,000	400.00
1855-S	6,600	500.00	1873	About 100 proofs	Rare
1856	26,000	400.00	1874	41,800	375.00
1856-S	34,500	450.00	1875	About 50 proofs	Rare
1857	20,900	325.00	1876	About 50 proofs	Rare
1857-S	14,000	400.00	1877	1,500	600.00
1858	2,100	500.00	1878	82,300	375.00
1859	15,600	350.00	1879	3,000	500.00
1860	7,200	400.00	1880	1,000	500.00
1860-S	7,000	400.00	1881	550	800.00
1861	6,100	400.00	1882	1,500	600.00
1862	5,800	400.00	1883	900	600.00
1863	5,000	400.00	1884	1,100	600.00
1864	2,700	425.00	1885	900	600.00
1865	1,200	500.00	1886	1,100	600.00
1866	4,000	400.00	1887	6,200	450.00
1867	2,600	400.00	1888	5,300	450.00
1868	4,900	400.00	1889	2,400	450.00
1869	2,500	400.00			

4 DOLLAR GOLD PIECES (STELLAS)

Type: Liberty head with flowing hair.

Date	Amount Minted	Value	Date	Amount Minted	Value
1879	415 proofs	**12,500.00**	1880	15 proofs	**Rare**

Type: Liberty head with coiled hair.

Date	Amount Minted	Value	Date	Amount Minted	Value
1879	10 proofs	**Rare**	1880	10 proofs	**Rare**

5 DOLLAR GOLD PIECES (HALF EAGLES)

Type: Liberty head; with small eagle on Rev.

Date	Amount Minted	Value	Date	Amount Minted	Value
1795	Part of 8,700	**3,000.00**	1797	Part of 6,400	**5,000.00**
1796	3,400	**4,000.00**	1798	Part of 24,900	—

Type: Liberty head to right; with large eagle on Rev.

Date	Amount Minted	Value	Date	Amount Minted	Value
1795	Part of 8,700	2,500.00	1803	33,500	750.00
1797	Part of 6,400	4,000.00	1804	30,500	750.00
1798	Part of 24,900	750.00	1805	33,200	750.00
1799	7,500	800.00	1806	64,100	750.00
1800	11,600	750.00	1807	Part of 84,100	800.00
1802	53,200	750.00			

Type: Draped bust of Liberty to left with round cap.

Date	Amount Minted	Value	Date	Amount Minted	Value
1807	Part of 84,100	800.00	1810	100,300	750.00
1808	55,600	750.00	1811	99,600	750.00
1809	33,900	750.00	1812	58,100	750.00

Type: Liberty head with round cap; with motto over eagle.

Date	Amount Minted	Value	Date	Amount Minted	Value
1813	95,400	900.00	1825	29,100	2,500.00
1814	15,500	1,000.00	1826	18,100	2,000.00
1815	635	Rare	1827	24,900	3,000.00
1818	48,600	900.00	1828	28,000	Rare
1819	51,700	Rare	1829	57,400	20,000.00
1820	263,800	900.00	1830	126,400	2,400.00
1821	34,600	1,500.00	1831	140,600	2,400.00
1822 (3 known)	17,800	Very Rare	1832	157,500	2,600.00
1823	14,500	1,200.00	1833	193,600	2,400.00
1824	17,300	1,750.00	1834	Part of 732,200	2,400.00

Type: Liberty head with ribbon; without motto over eagle.

(The mint marks are on the Obv., over the date)

Date	Amount Minted	Value	Date	Amount Minted	Value
	Part of 732,200	**175.00**	1838	286,600	**175.00**
1834	371,500	**175.00**	1838-C	12,900	**1,000.00**
1835	553,100	**175.00**	1838-D	20,600	**900.00**
1836	207,100	**175.00**			
1837					

Type: Liberty head with coronet; without motto over eagle.

(The mint marks are on the Rev., under the eagle)

Date	Amount Minted	Value	Date	Amount Minted	Value
1839	118,100	**150.00**	1847-D	64,400	**300.00**
1839-C	23,500	**300.00**	1848	260,800	**110.00**
1839-D	18,900	**250.00**	1848-C	64,500	**275.00**
1840	137,400	**120.00**	1848-D	47,500	**350.00**
1840-O	30,400	**150.00**	1849	133,100	**110.00**
1840-C	19,000	**300.00**	1849-C	64,800	**250.00**
1840-D	22,900	**300.00**	1849-D	39,000	**250.00**
1841	15,800	**160.00**	1850	64,500	**150.00**
1841-O	8,300	**—**	1850-C	63,600	**250.00**
1841-C	21,500	**250.00**	1850-D	43,900	**250.00**
1841-D	30,500	**265.00**	1851	377,500	**100.00**
1842	27,600	**110.00**	1851-O	41,000	**250.00**
1842-O	16,400	**250.00**	1851-C	49,200	**250.00**
1842-C	27,500	**250.00**	1851-D	62,700	**275.00**
1842-D	59,600	**250.00**	1852	573,900	**100.00**
1843	611,200	**100.00**	1852-C	72,600	**250.00**
1843-O	101,100	**140.00**	1852-D	91,500	**250.00**
1843-C	44,400	**275.00**	1853	305,800	**100.00**
1843-D	98,500	**275.00**	1853-C	65,600	**300.00**
1844	340,300	**100.00**	1853-D	89,700	**275.00**
1844-O	364,600	**140.00**	1854	160,700	**120.00**
1844-C	23,600	**450.00**	1854-O	46,000	**150.00**
1844-D	89,000	**400.00**	1854-C	39,300	**325.00**
1845	417,100	**110.00**	1854-D	56,400	**300.00**
1845-O	41,000	**150.00**	1854-S	268	**—**
1845-D	90,600	**275.00**	1855	117,100	**100.00**
1846	395,900	**110.00**	1855-O	1,100	**275.00**
1846-O	58,000	**120.00**	1855-C	39,800	**275.00**
1846-C	13,000	**350.00**	1855-D	22,400	**325.00**
1846-D	80,300	**300.00**	1855-S	61,000	**120.00**
1847	916,000	**100.00**	1856	198,000	**100.00**
1847-O	12,000	**375.00**	1856-O	10,000	**325.00**
1847-C	84,200	**275.00**	1856-C	28,500	**160.00**

Date	Amount Minted	Value	Date	Amount Minted	Value
1856-D	19,800	300.00	1860-C	14,800	250.00
1856-S	105,100	140.00	1860-D	14,600	250.00
1857	98,200	100.00	1860-S	21,200	325.00
1857-O	13,000	200.00	1861	639,900	100.00
1857-C	31,400	200.00	1861-C	6,900	550.00
1857-D	17,000	200.00	1861-D	1,600	2,100.00
1857-S	87,000	150.00	1861-S	18,000	350.00
1858	15,100	150.00	1862	4,500	325.00
1858-C	38,900	325.00	1862-S	9,500	1,200.00
1858-D	15,400	250.00	1863	2,500	400.00
1858-S	18,600	300.00	1863-S	17,000	325.00
1859	16,800	150.00	1864	4,200	300.00
1859-C	31,800	220.00	1864-S	3,900	2,000.00
1859-D	10,400	325.00	1865	1,300	500.00
1859-S	13,200	325.00	1865-S	27,600	350.00
1860	19,800	130.00	1866-S	Part of 43,900	475.00

Type: Liberty head with coronet; with motto over eagle.

(The mint marks are on the Rev., under the eagle)

Date	Amount Minted	Value	Date	Amount Minted	Value
1866	6,700	400.00	1878	131,700	125.00
1866-S	Part of 43,900	500.00	1878-S	144,700	150.00
1867	6,900	350.00	1878-CC	9,100	6,000.00
1867-S	29,000	450.00	1879	301,900	90.00
1868	5,700	400.00	1879-S	426,200	90.00
1868-S	52,000	325.00	1879-CC	17,300	525.00
1869	1,800	500.00	1880	3¼ million	90.00
1869-S	31,000	350.00	1880-S	1⅓ million	90.00
1870	4,000	400.00	1880-CC	51,000	500.00
1870-S	17,000	600.00	1881	5⅔ million	90.00
1870-CC	7,700	2,250.00	1881-S	969,000	90.00
1871	3,200	450.00	1881-CC	13,900	225.00
1871-S	25,000	350.00	1882	2½ million	90.00
1871-CC	20,800	500.00	1882-S	970,000	90.00
1872	1,700	400.00	1882-CC	82,800	500.00
1872-S	36,400	200.00	1883	233,400	90.00
1872-CC	17,000	400.00	1883-S	83,200	110.00
1873	112,500	100.00	1883-CC	13,000	225.00
1873-S	31,000	400.00	1884	191,000	90.00
1873-CC	7,400	750.00	1884-S	177,000	100.00
1874	3,500	350.00	1884-CC	16,400	500.00
1874-S	16,000	350.00	1885	601,500	90.00
1874-CC	21,200	400.00	1885-S	1¼ million	90.00
1875	220	Very Rare	1886	388,400	80.00
1875-S	9,000	400.00	1886-S	3¼ million	90.00
1875-CC	11,800	700.00	1887	87 proofs	Rare
1876	1,500	500.00	1887-S	2 million	90.00
1876-S	4,000	750.00	1888	18,300	125.00
1876-CC	6,900	500.00	1888-S	293,900	125.00
1877	1,200	450.00	1889	7,600	150.00
1877-S	26,700	200.00	1890	4,300	400.00
1877-CC	8,700	700.00	1890-CC	53,800	175.00

Date	Amount Minted	Value	Date	Amount Minted	Value
1891	61,400	110.00	1899	1 3/4 million	90.00
1891-CC	208,000	195.00	1899-S	1 1/2 million	90.00
1892	753,600	90.00	1900	1 1/3 million	90.00
1892-O	10,000	700.00	1900-S	329,000	110.00
1892-S	298,400	95.00	1901	616,000	90.00
1892-CC	83,000	300.00	1901-S	3 2/3 million	90.00
1893	1 1/2 million	90.00	1902	172,600	90.00
1893-O	110,000	110.00	1902-S	939,000	90.00
1893-S	224,000	100.00	1903	227,000	90.00
1893-CC	60,000	150.00	1903-S	1 3/4 million	90.00
1894	958,000	90.00	1904	392,100	90.00
1894-O	16,600	175.00	1904-S	97,000	100.00
1894-S	55,900	175.00	1905	302,300	90.00
1895	1 1/3 million	90.00	1905-S	880,700	100.00
1895-S	112,000	175.00	1906	348,800	90.00
1896	59,100	90.00	1906-S	598,000	90.00
1896-S	155,400	160.00	1906-D	320,000	90.00
1897	867,900	90.00	1907	626,200	90.00
1897-S	354,000	120.00	1907-D	888,000	90.00
1898	633,500	90.00	1908	421,900	90.00
1898-S	1 1/3 million	90.00			

Type: Indian head.

(The mint marks are on the Rev., to the left of the value)

Date	Amount Minted	Value	Date	Amount Minted	Value
1908	578,000	125.00	1911-S	1 1/2 million	140.00
1908-D	148,000	125.00	1912	790,100	125.00
1908-S	82,000	320.00	1912-S	392,000	140.00
1909	627,100	125.00	1913	916,100	125.00
1909-O	34,200	650.00	1913-S	408,000	140.00
1909-D	3 1/2 million	125.00	1914	247,100	125.00
1909-S	297,200	140.00	1914-D	247,000	125.00
1910	604,200	125.00	1914-S	263,000	140.00
1910-D	193,600	125.00	1915	588,100	140.00
1910-S	770,200	140.00	1915-S	164,000	220.00
1911	915,100	125.00	1916-S	240,000	140.00
1911-D	72,500	300.00	1929	662,000	2,500.00

10 DOLLAR GOLD PIECES (EAGLES)

Type: Liberty head; with small eagle on Rev.

Date	Amount Minted	Value	Date	Amount Minted	Value
1795	2,800	**4,000.00**	1797	Part of 9,200	**4,000.00**
1796	6,100	**4,000.00**			

Type: Liberty head; with large eagle on Rev.

Date	Amount Minted	Value	Date	Amount Minted	Value
1797	Part of 9,200	**1,300.00**	1801	29,300	**1,200.00**
1798	8,000	**3,000.00**	1803	9,000	**1,250.00**
1799	17,500	**1,100.00**	1804	9,800	**2,000.00**
1800	26,000	**1,200.00**			

Type: Liberty head; without motto on Rev.
(The mint marks are on the Rev., under the eagle)

Date	Amount Minted	Value	Date	Amount Minted	Value
1838	7,200	**400.00**	1842	81,500	**200.00**
1839	38,200	**300.00**	1842-O	27,400	**200.00**
1840	47,300	**225.00**	1843	75,500	**200.00**
1841	63,100	**200.00**	1843-O	175,200	**200.00**
1841-O	2,500	**700.00**	1844	6,400	**350.00**

Date	Amount Minted	Value	Date	Amount Minted	Value
1844-O	118,700	200.00	1856-O	14,500	325.00
1845	26,200	200.00	1856-S	68,000	150.00
1845-O	47,500	200.00	1857	16,600	225.00
1846	20,100	400.00	1857-O	5,500	550.00
1846-O	81,800	250.00	1857-S	26,000	225.00
1847	862,300	175.00	1858	2,500	2,000.00
1847-O	571,500	175.00	1858-O	20,000	200.00
1848	145,500	180.00	1858-S	11,800	625.00
1848-O	35,800	275.00	1859	16,100	225.00
1849	653,600	150.00	1859-O	2,300	1,000.00
1849-O	23,900	400.00	1859-S	7,000	750.00
1850	291,500	150.00	1860	11,800	225.00
1850-O	57,500	210.00	1860-O	11,100	275.00
1851	176,300	150.00	1860-S	5,000	600.00
1851-O	263,000	150.00	1861	113,200	160.00
1852	263,100	180.00	1861-S	15,500	500.00
1852-O	18,000	350.00	1862	11,000	250.00
1853	201,300	150.00	1862-S	12,500	550.00
1853-O	51,000	175.00	1863	1,200	1,600.00
1854	54,200	200.00	1863-S	10,000	550.00
1854-O	52,500	175.00	1864	3,600	625.00
1854-S	123,800	150.00	1864-S	2,500	2,250.00
1855	121,700	150.00	1865	4,000	600.00
1855-O	18,000	375.00	1865-S	16,700	1,200.00
1855-S	9,000	600.00	1866-S	Part of 20,000	1,100.00
1856	60,500	160.00			

Type: Liberty head; with motto on Rev.

(The mint marks are on the Rev., under the eagle)

Date	Amount Minted	Value	Date	Amount Minted	Value
1866	3,800	400.00	1874	53,200	180.00
1866-S	Part of 20,000	750.00	1874-S	10,000	800.00
1867	3,100	800.00	1874-CC	16,800	400.00
1867-S	9,000	1,400.00	1875	120	—
1868	10,700	375.00	1875-CC	7,700	1,250.00
1868-S	13,500	750.00	1876	732	1,500.00
1869	1,900	750.00	1876-S	5,000	800.00
1869-S	6,400	750.00	1876-CC	4,700	1,100.00
1870	2,500	500.00	1877	817	1,250.00
1870-S	8,000	800.00	1877-S	17,000	250.00
1870-CC	5,900	3,500.00	1877-CC	3,300	1,100.00
1871	1,800	700.00	1878	73,800	180.00
1871-S	16,500	700.00	1878-S	26,100	450.00
1871-CC	7,200	750.00	1878-CC	3,200	1,750.00
1872	1,600	1,400.00	1879	384,800	180.00
1872-S	17,300	500.00	1879-O	1,500	1,100.00
1872-CC	5,500	1,000.00	1879-S	224,000	180.00
1873	825	2,400.00	1879-CC	1,800	2,000
1873-S	12,000	750.00	1880	1²/₃ million	180.00
1873-CC	4,500	1,200.00	1880-O	9,200	200.00

Date	Amount Minted	Value	Date	Amount Minted	Value
1880-S	506,200	180.00	1893-CC	14,000	180.00
1880-CC	11,200	250.00	1894	2½ million	180.00
1881	3¾ million	180.00	1894-O	107,500	180.00
1881-O	8,300	200.00	1894-S	25,000	180.00
1881-S	970,000	180.00	1895	567,800	180.00
1881-CC	24,000	200.00	1895-O	98,000	180.00
1882	2⅓ million	180.00	1895-S	49,000	180.00
1882-O	10,800	200.00	1896	76,300	180.00
1882-S	132,000	180.00	1896-S	123,700	180.00
1882-CC	6,800	300.00	1897	1 million	180.00
1883	208,700	180.00	1897-O	42,500	180.00
1883-O	800	1,250.00	1897-S	234,700	180.00
1883-S	38,000	185.00	1898	812,200	180.00
1883-CC	12,000	275.00	1898-S	473,600	180.00
1884	76,900	180.00	1899	1¼ million	180.00
1884-S	124,200	180.00	1899-O	37,000	180.00
1884-CC	9,900	300.00	1899-S	841,000	180.00
1885	253,500	180.00	1900	294,000	180.00
1885-S	228,000	180.00	1900-S	81,000	180.00
1886	236,200	180.00	1901	1¾ million	180.00
1886-S	826,000	180.00	1901-O	72,000	180.00
1887	53,700	180.00	1901-S	2¾ million	180.00
1887-S	817,000	180.00	1902	82,500	180.00
1888	133,000	180.00	1902-S	469,500	180.00
1888-O	21,300	180.00	1903	125,900	180.00
1888-S	648,700	180.00	1903-O	112,800	180.00
1889	4,500	180.00	1903-S	538,000	180.00
1889-S	425,400	180.00	1904	162,000	180.00
1890	58,000	180.00	1904-O	108,900	180.00
1890-CC	17,500	200.00	1905	201,000	180.00
1891	91,900	180.00	1905-S	369,200	180.00
1891-CC	103,700	190.00	1906	165,500	180.00
1892	797,600	180.00	1906-O	86,900	180.00
1892-O	28,700	180.00	1906-S	457,000	180.00
1892-S	115,500	180.00	906-D	981,000	180.00
1892-CC	40,000	200.00	1907	1¼ million	180.00
1893	1¾ million	180.00	1907-S	210,500	180.00
1893-O	17,000	180.00	1907-D	1 million	210.00
1893-S	141,300	180.00			

Type: Indian head; without motto on Rev.

(The Mint marks are on the Rev., to the left of the value. The "1907 Periods" indicates a period at each end of "United States of America" on the Rev.)

Date	Amount Minted	Value	Date	Amount Minted	Value
1907	239,400	250.00	1908	33,500	325.00
1907 Periods	542	3,000.00	1908-D	210,000	335.00

Type: Indian head; with motto on Rev.

Date	Amount Minted	Value	Date	Amount Minted	Value
1908	341,500	**300.00**	1913	442,100	**300.00**
1908-D	836,500	**325.00**	1913-S	66,000	**450.00**
1908-S	59,900	**425.00**	1914	151,000	**300.00**
1909	184,900	**300.00**	1914-D	343,500	**300.00**
1909-D	121,500	**325.00**	1914-S	208,000	**300.00**
1909-S	292,300	**325.00**	1915	351,100	**300.00**
1910	318,700	**300.00**	1915-S	59,000	**400.00**
1910-D	2⅓ million	**300.00**	1916-S	138,500	**325.00**
1910-S	811,000	**300.00**	1920-S	126,500	**4,500.00**
1911	505,600	**300.00**	1926	1 million	**300.00**
1911-D	30,100	**400.00**	1930-S	96,000	**4,000.00**
1911-S	51,000	**350.00**	1932	4½ million	**300.00**
1912	405,000	**300.00**	1933	312,500	—
1912-S	300,000	**310.00**			

20 DOLLAR GOLD PIECES (DOUBLE EAGLES)

Type: Liberty head; without motto on Rev.
(The mint marks are on the Rev., under the eagle)

Date	Amount Minted	Value	Date	Amount Minted	Value
1850	1¼ million	**325.00**	1856	329,900	**360.00**
1850-O	141,000	**350.00**	1856-O	2,200	—
1851	2 million	**325.00**	1856-S	1¼ million	**325.00**
1851-O	315,000	**350.00**	1857	439,400	**350.00**
1852	2 million	**325.00**	1857-O	30,000	**600.00**
1852-O	190,000	**360.00**	1857-S	970,500	**325.00**
1853	1¼ million	**300.00**	1858	211,700	**500.00**
1853-O	71,000	**325.00**	1858-O	35,200	**650.00**
1854	757,900	**325.00**	1858-S	846,700	**325.00**
1854-O	3,200	—	1859	43,600	**450.00**
1854-S	141,500	**350.00**	1859-O	9,100	**1,500.00**
1855	364,700	**350.00**	1859-S	636,400	**360.00**
1855-O	8,000	**1,200.00**	1860	577,700	**325.00**
1855-S	879,700	**325.00**	1860-O	6,600	**1,750.00**

Date	Amount Minted	Value	Date	Amount Minted	Value
1860-S	544,900	400.00	1863-S	966,600	375.00
1861	3 million	375.00	1864	204,300	400.00
1861-O	5,000	1,000.00	1864-S	793,700	400.00
1861-S	768,000	425.00	1865	351,200	375.00
1862	92,100	600.00	1865-S	1 million	375.00
1862-S	854,200	400.00	1866-S	Part of 842,200	750.00
1863	142,800	400.00			

Type: Liberty head; with motto on Rev. and "Twenty D."

(The mint marks are on the Rev., under the eagle)

Date	Amounted Minted	Value	Date	Amount Minted	Value
1866	698,800	375.00	1872-S	780,000	360.00
1866-S	Part of 842,200	400.00	1872-CC	29,600	625.00
1867	251,065	360.00	1873	1¾ million	360.00
1867-S	920,700	375.00	1873-S	1 million	375.00
1868	98,600	450.00	1873-CC	22,400	700.00
1868-S	837,500	360.00	1874	366,800	360.00
1869	171,200	375.00	1874-S	1¼ million	360.00
1869-S	686,700	375.00	1874-CC	115,100	400.00
1870	155,200	400.00	1875	295,700	360.00
1870-S	382,000	360.00	1875-S	1¼ million	360.00
1870-CC	3,800	—	1875-CC	111,100	400.00
1871	80,100	400.00	1876	583,900	360.00
1871-S	928,000	360.00	1876-S	1½ million	360.00
1871-CC	14,700	1,200	1876-CC	138,400	425.00
1872	251,900	360.00			

Type: Liberty head; with motto on Rev. and "Twenty Dollars."

(The mint marks are on the Rev., under the eagle)

Date	Amount Minted	Value	Date	Amount Minted	Value
1877	397,700	360.00	1878	543,600	360.00
1877-S	1¾ million	360.00	1878-S	1¾ million	360.00
1877-CC	42,600	400.00	1878-CC	13,200	535.00

Date	Amount Minted	Value	Date	Amount Minted	Value
1879	207,600	**360.00**	1892-S	930,100	**360.00**
1879-O	2,300	**1,500.00**	1892-CC	27,300	**400.00**
1879-S	1¼ million	**360.00**	1893	344,300	**360.00**
1879-CC	10,700	**550.00**	1893-S	996,200	**360.00**
1880	51,500	**360.00**	1893-CC	18,400	**425.00**
1880-S	836,000	**360.00**	1894	1½ million	**360.00**
1881	2,300	**2,000.00**	1894-S	1 million	**360.00**
1881-S	727,000	**360.00**	1895	1 million	**360.00**
1882	630	**4,000.00**	1895-S	1¼ million	**360.00**
1882-S	1¼ million	**360.00**	1896	792,700	**360.00**
1882-CC	39,100	**425.00**	1896-S	1½ million	**360.00**
1883	About 100 proofs	—	1897	1⅓ million	**360.00**
1883-S	1¼ million	**360.00**	1897-S	1½ million	**360.00**
1883-CC	60,000	**400.00**	1898	170,500	**360.00**
1884	71 proofs	—	1898-S	2½ million	**360.00**
1884-S	916,000	**360.00**	1899	1⅔ million	**360.00**
1884-CC	81,100	**420.00**	1899-S	2 million	**360.00**
1885	828	**4,000.00**	1900	1¾ million	**360.00**
1885-S	683,500	**360.00**	1900-S	2½ million	**360.00**
1885-CC	9,500	**550.00**	1901	111,500	**360.00**
1886	1,100	**4,000.00**	1901-S	1½ million	**360.00**
1887	121 proofs	—	1902	31,300	**360.00**
1887-S	283,000	**360.00**	1902-S	1¾ million	**360.00**
1888	226,300	**360.00**	1903	287,400	**360.00**
1888-S	859,600	**360.00**	1903-S	954,000	**360.00**
1889	44,100	**360.00**	1904	6¼ million	**360.00**
1889-S	774,700	**360.00**	1904-S	5¼ million	**360.00**
1889-CC	30,900	**450.00**	1905	59,000	**360.00**
1890	76,000	**360.00**	1905-S	1¾ million	**360.00**
1890-S	802,700	**360.00**	1906	69,700	**360.00**
1890-CC	91,200	**425.00**	1906-S	2 million	**360.00**
1891	1,400	**1,000.00**	1906-D	620,200	**360.00**
1891-S	1¼ million	**360.00**	1907	1½ million	**360.00**
1891-CC	5,000	**800.00**	1907-S	2¼ million	**360.00**
1892	4,500	**600.00**	1907-D	842,200	**360.00**

Type: Liberty standing (St. Gaudens design).
Date in Roman Numerals, MCMVII.

Date	Amount Minted	Value
1907	11,200	**2,250.00**

Type: Liberty standing; date in normal numerals; without motto on Rev.

(The mint mark is on the Obv., over the date)

Date	Amount Minted	Value	Date	Amount Minted	Value
1907	361,700	**375.00**	1908-D	663,700	**360.00**
1908	4¼ million	**360.00**			

Type: Liberty standing; with motto on Rev.

(The mint marks are on the Obv., over the date)

Date	Amount Minted	Value	Date	Amount Minted	Value
1908	156,400	**360.00**	1922	1⅓ million	**360.00**
1908-D	349,500	**360.00**	1922-S	2⅔ million	**400.00**
1908-S	22,000	**650.00**	1923	566,000	**360.00**
1909	Part of 161,300	**360.00**	1923-D	1⅔ million	**360.00**
1909 over 8	Part of 161,300	**360.00**	1924	4⅓ million	**360.00**
1909-D	52,500	**450.00**	1924-D	3 million	**725.00**
1909-S	2¾ million	**360.00**	1924-S	3 million	**600.00**
1910	482,200	**360.00**	1925	2¾ million	**360.00**
1910-D	429,000	**360.00**	1925-D	3 million	**650.00**
1910-S	2¼ million	**360.00**	1925-S	3¾ million	**600.00**
1911	197,300	**360.00**	1926	816,700	**360.00**
1911-D	846,500	**360.00**	1926-D	481,000	**1,600.00**
1911-S	775,700	**360.00**	1926-S	2 million	**600.00**
1912	149,800	**360.00**	1927	3 million	**360.00**
1913	168,800	**360.00**	1927-D	180,000	**—**
1913-D	393,500	**360.00**	1927-S	3 million	**2,500.00**
1913-S	34,000	**375.00**	1928	8¾ million	**360.00**
1914	95,300	**375.00**	1929	1¾ million	**5,000.00**
1914-D	453,000	**360.00**	1930-S	74,000	**6,500.00**
1914-S	1½ million	**360.00**	1931	3 million	**6,000.00**
1915	152,000	**360.00**	1931-D	106,500	**5,000.00**
1915-S	567,500	**360.00**	1932	1 million	**6,500.00**
1916-S	796,000	**360.00**	1933	445,500	**not issued**
1920	228,200	**360.00**			
1920-S	558,000	**4,500.00**			
1921	528,500	**6,500.00**			

THE AMERICAN EAGLES

These coins were approved by Congress and first released by the mint in the fall of 1986. Although each coin bears a denomination, the uncirculated versions are bought and sold strictly on the basis of their gold or silver content and bullion prices at the time of the transaction. The proof versions were intended for collectors and were sold by the mint at a premium over bullion content.

Type: Silver Eagle

Denomination	Date	Unc	Proof
1 Dollar: Gold Eagles	1986	7.50	10.00
1 Dollar: Gold Eagles	1987	4.50	12.00
1 Dollar: Gold Eagles	1988	4.50	45.00
1 Dollar: Gold Eagles	1989	5.00	12.00
1 Dollar: Gold Eagles	1990	4.50	15.00
1 Dollar: Gold Eagles	1991	4.50	13.50
1 Dollar: Gold Eagles	1992	4.50	12.00
	1993	6.50	22.50
5 Dollars (¹/₁₀ oz)	1986	34.00	none
	1987	34.00	none
	1988	34.00	37.50
	1989	34.00	45.00
	1990	34.00	37.50
	1991	34.00	40.00
	1992	34.00	42.00
	1993	34.00	50.00
10 Dollars (¹/₄ oz)	1986	80.00	none
	1987	80.00	none
	1988	80.00	95.00
	1989	95.00	95.00
	1990	80.00	95.00
	1991	80.00	95.00
	1992	85.00	100.00
	1993	110.00	140.00
25 dollars (¹/₂ oz)	1986	175.00	none
	1987	175.00	200.00
	1988	175.00	200.00
	1989	175.00	210.00
	1990	275.00	215.00
	1991	225.00	200.00
	1992	175.00	200.00
	1993	175.00	225.00
50 Dollars (1 oz)	1986	360.00	370.00
	1987	360.00	370.00
	1988	360.00	370.00
	1989	360.00	375.00
	1990	360.00	375.00
	1991	360.00	365.00
	1992	360.00	415.00
	1993	360.00	370.00

Pioneer Gold Coins

Coinage of the Territorial and Private Mints

(The valuations are for coins in VG to F condition)
(Beware of Copies)

BALDWIN & CO.
San Francisco, California

Horseman with lariat. Rev. Eagle.

10 Dollars 1850 . . . . **7,500.00**

"Baldwin & Co" on head band of Liberty. Rev. Eagle.

5 Dollars 1850 . . . . **1,750.00**
10 Dollars 1851 . . . . **3,500.00**
20 Dollars 1851 . . . . ——

AUGUST BECHTLER
Rutherford, North Carolina

Value and legend. Rev. Weight and legend. The coins are undated but were struck from
1842 to 1852.

1 Dollar ND. One variety **400.00**
5 Dollars ND. Three varieties **1,500.00**

CHRISTOPHER BECHTLER
Rutherford, North Carolina

Value and legend. Rev. Weight and legend. The coins are undated, but were struck from 1831 to 1842.

1 Dollar ND. Four varieties	**600.00**
2½ Dollars ND. Seven varieties	**1,000.00**
5 Dollars ND. Six varieties	**1,500.00**
5 Dollars August 1, 1834. Two varieties	**1,500.00**

EPHRAIM BRASHER
New York

Radiant sun over mountains. Rev. Eagle with "EB" punched on either the wing or breast. The famous Brasher Doubloon.

Doubloon 1787 Extremely Rare	——
1/2 Doubloon 1787 Extremely Rare	——

CINCINNATI MINING & TRADING CO.
San Francisco, California

Indian Head. Rev. Eagle

5 Dollars 1849	——
10 Dollars 1849	——

CLARK, GRUBER & CO.
Denver, Colorado

View of Pikes Peak. Rev. Eagle

10 Dollars 1860	**1,500.00**
20 Dollars 1860	**12,000.00**

"Clark & Co. on head band of Liberty. Rev. Eagle.

2¹/₂ Dollars 1860	**450.00**
5 Dollars 1860	**600.00**

"Pikes Peak" on head band of Liberty. Rev. Eagle.

2¹/₂ Dollars 1861	**400.00**
5 Dollars 1861	**500.00**
10 Dollars 1861	**500.00**
20 Dollars 1861	**1,250.00**

J. J. CONWAY & CO.
Georgia Gulch, Colorado

Name of company. Rev. Value and "Pikes Peak." Undated but struck in 1861.

2½ Dollars ND . . . . —
5   Dollars ND . . . . —
10 Dollars ND . . . . —

DUBOSQ & CO.
San Francisco, California

"Dubosq & Co." on head band of Liberty. Rev. Eagle.

5 Dollars 1850 . . . . —
10 Dollars 1850 . . . . —

DUNBAR & CO.
San Francisco, California

"Dunbar & Co." on head band of Liberty. Rev. Eagle

5 Dollars 1851 . . . . —

AUGUSTUS HUMBERT
U.S. Assayer of gold, San Francisco, California

Eagle. Rev. Four line legend in tablet.

10 Dollars 1852 . . . . **1,000.00**
20 Dollars 1852 . . . . **1,250.00**

Eagle. Rev. Small 50, star or circle in center of otherwise blank Rev. Octagonal shaped with lettered edge.

50 Dollars 1851. Five varieties **3,500.00**

Eagle. Rev. Machine made criss-cross of circular lines. Octagonal shaped with reeded edge.

50 Dollars 1851, 52. Three varieties **3,500.00**

KELLOGG & CO.
San Francisco, California

"Kellogg & Co." on head band of Liberty. Rev. Standard Eagle.

20 Dollars 1854, 55 . . . . **700.00**

Obv. Similar to above. Rev. Eagle holding shield.

50 Dollars 1855 . . . . ——

MASSACHUSETTS & CALIFORNIA CO.
San Francisco, California

Arms supported by bear and stag. Value in wreath.

5 Dollars 1849. Four varieties . . . . ——

MINERS BANK
San Francisco, California

Name and value. Rev. Eagle.

10 Dollars 1849 . . . . **2,000.00**

MOFFAT & CO.
San Francisco, California

"Moffat & Co." on head band of Liberty. Rev. Eagle.

5 Dollars 1849, 50 . . . . **300.00**
10 Dollars 1849, 52 . . . . **650.00**
20 Dollars 1853 . . . . **800.00**

THE MORMONS
Salt Lake City, Utah

Eye and Bishop's Mitre. Rev. Clasped hands.

2½ Dollars 1849	. . . .	**1,200.00**
5 Dollars 1849, 50	. . . .	**1,000.00**
10 Dollars 1849	. . . .	——
20 Dollars 1849	. . . .	——

Lion. Rev. Beehive on breast of eagle.

5 Dollars 1860 . . . . **2,000.00**

NORRIS, GRIEG & NORRIS
San Francisco, California

Eagle. Rev. Legend.

5 Dollars 1849. Plain or reeded edge **950.00**

OREGON EXCHANGE CO.
Oregon City, Oregon

Beaver and initials. Rev. Legend.

5 Dollars 1849	**2,500.00**
10 Dollars 1849	**9,000.00**

J. S. ORMSBY
San Francisco, California

"J. S. O." Rev. Value. Undated but struck in 1849.

5 Dollars ND	—
10 Dollars ND	—

PACIFIC CO.
San Francisco, California

Liberty Cap. Rev. Eagle.

5 Dollars 1849	—
10 Dollars 1849	—

JOHN PARSONS & CO.
Tarryall Mines, Colorado

Stamping machine. Rev. Eagle and "Pikes Peak Gold." Undated but struck in 1861.

2½ Dollars ND . . . . —
5   Dollars ND . . . . —

SHULTS & CO.
San Francisco, California

"Shults & Co." on head band of Liberty. Rev. Eagle.

5 Dollars 1851 . . . . **4,000.00**

TEMPLETON REID
Lumpkin County, Georgia

Legend on each side.

2½ Dollars 1830 . . . . —
5   Dollars 1830 . . . . —
10 Dollars 1830 . . . . —
10 Dollars ND . . . . —

TEMPLETON REID
San Francisco, California

Legend on each side.

10 Dollars 1849 . . . . ⸻
25 Dollars 1849 . . . . ⸻

UNITED STATES ASSAY OFFICE OF GOLD
San Francisco, California

Eagle. Rev. Legend in tablet.

10 Dollars 1852, 53. Two varieties **500.00**
20 Dollars 1853. Two varieties **950.00**

Eagle. Rev. Machine made criss-cross of circular lines. Octagonal shaped.

50 Dollars 1852. Two varieties **2,500.00**

WASS, MOLITOR & CO.
San Francisco, California

"W.M. & Co." on head band of Liberty. Rev. Eagle.

5 Dollars 1852 . . . . **1,200.00**
10 Dollars 1852, 55. Two varieties **1,000.00**
20 Dollars. 1855. Two varieties **2,750.00**

Liberty head. Rev. Name and value.

50 Dollars 1855 . . . . **5,000.00**

United States Proof Sets
(1936 to date)

A Proof Set contains five coins; the lc, 5c, 25c, and 50c pieces. From 1936 through 1942, unequal amounts were struck of each denomination; from 1950 to date equal amounts have been struck. In the column under Amount Minted, the figure shows the total number of complete sets minted in each year. In 1942, two types of proof 5 Cent pieces were struck, the standard coin and the one with silver content; hence, there are two listings for the 1942 Proof Set. In 1973 and 1974, the dollar was added to the set. in 1975, the Proof Set contained the 1975-S lc, 5c and 10c pieces plus the 1976-S Bicentennial 25c, 50c and dollar. Because of speculation, the valuations are subject to fluctuation.

Date	Amount Minted	Value	Date	Amount Minted	Value
1936	3,837	2,400.00	1978-S	3,127,781	6.00
1937	5,542	1,400.00	1979 Type I	3,677,175	6.00
1938	8,045	700.00	1979 Type II		45.00
1939	8,795	700.00	1980-S	3,547,030	5.00
1940	11,246	500.00	1981 Type I	4,063,083	5.00
1941	15,287	450.00	1981 Type II		150.00
1942 with one nickel	21,120	400.00	1982-S	3,857,479	4.00
1942 with two nickels		450.00	1983-S	3,183,765	5.00
1950	51,386	300.00	1983 Prestige	140,361	60.00
1951	57,500	200.00	1984-S	2,748,430	8.00
1952	81,980	100.00	1984 Prestige	316,680	30.00
1953	128,800	75.00	1985-S	3,362,821	5.00
1954	233,300	40.00	1986-S	2,411,180	15.00
1955	378,200	42.50	1986 Prestige	599,317	23.00
1956	669,384	20.00	987-S	3,356,738	4.00
1957	1,247,952	10.00	1987 Prestige	435,495	20.00
1958	875,652	13.00	1988-S	3,031,287	8.00
1959	1,149,291	10.00	1988 Prestige	231,661	35.00
1960 small date	1,691,600	12.50	1989-S	3,220,194	6.50
1960 large date		7.00	1989-S Prestige	211,087	40.00
1961	3,028,244	6.00	1990-S		12.00
1962	3,218,039	6.00	1990-S Prestige	2,793,433	25.00
1963	3,075,645	6.00	1991-S	506,125	12.50
1964	3,949,634	6.00	1991-S Prestige	2,610,833	65.00
1965 special mint set	2,360,000	3.00	1992-S	2,675,688	12.00
1966 special mint set	2,261,583	3.50	1992-S Prestige	83,293	40.00
1967 special mint set	1,863,344	4.00	1992-S 90% Silver	1,317,579	15.00
1968-S proof set	3,041,509	3.00	1992-S Silver Prem.	Part of above	22.50
1969-5	2,934,631	3.00	1993-S	2,409,394	10.00
1970 small date	2,632,810	20.00	1993-S 90% Silver	224,045	37.50
1970 large date		6.00	1993-S 90% Silver	570,213	12.50
1971-S	3,224,138	3.00	1994-S		9.00
1972-S	3,267,667	3.00	1994-S Prestige		35.00
1973-S	2,769,624	4.00	1994-S 90% Silver		11.00
1974-S	2,617,350	4.00			
1975-S	2,845,451	5.00			
1976-S 3-pc. set	3,295,715	7.00			
1976-S	4,149,730	5.00			
1977-S	3,251,152	5.00			

United States Paper Money
(1861 to date)

LARGE SIZE NOTES, SMALL SIZE NOTES, FRACTIONAL CURRENCY
1 DOLLAR NOTES

Torn, frayed or excessively worn notes command little or no premium.
All modern Federal Reserve Notes after 1974 have no premium.

Type of Issue	Series	Portrait or Main Design	Value
LARGE SIZE NOTES			**USED CONDITION**
U.S. Note (Legal Tender)	1862	Chase	30.00
"	1869	Washington	35.00
"	1874	Washington	15.00
"	1875	Washington	9.00
"	1878	Washington	9.00
"	1880	Washington	10.00
"	1917	Washington	7.50
"	1923	Washington (Red Seal)	8.00
Silver Certificate	1886	Martha Washington	16.00
"	1891	Martha Washington	15.00
"	1896	George and Martha Washington (on Rev.)	50.00
"	1899	Lincoln and Grant	9.50
"	1923	Washington (Blue Seal)	4.00
Treasury or Coin Note	1890	Stanton	10.00
"	1891	Stanton	10.00
National Bank Note	Old (original)	Two maidens standing	50.00
"	1875	Two maidens standing	50.00
Federal Reserve Bank Note	1918	Washington	5.00
SMALL SIZE NOTES			**NEW CONDITION**
U.S. Note (Red Seal)	1928	Washington	20.00
Silver Certificate (Blue Seal)	1928 (A-E)	Washington	5.00
"	1934	Washington	3.00
Silver Certificate (Blue Seal)	1935 (A-H*)	Washington	1.25
"	1957 (A-B)	Washington	1.15
Hawaiian Issue (Brown Seal)	1935-A	Washington	15.00
Armed Forces Issue (Yellow Seal)	1935-A	Washington	15.00
Federal Reserve (Green Seal)	1963 (A-B)	Washington	1.00
"	1969 (A-D)	Washington	1.00
"	1974 & later	Washington	Current

*1935-G with and without motto

2 DOLLAR NOTES

Torn, frayed or excessively worn notes command little or no premium.
All modern Federal Reserve Notes after 1974 have no premium.

Type of Issue	Series	Portrait or Main Design	Value
LARGE SIZE NOTES			**USED CONDITION**
U.S. Note (Legal Tender)	1862	Hamilton	25.00
"	1869	Jefferson	37.50
"	1874	Jefferson	25.00
"	1875	Jefferson	20.00
"	1878	Jefferson	20.00
"	1880	Jefferson	15.00
"	1917	Jefferson	10.00

Type of Issue	Series	Portrait or Main Design	Value
LARGE SIZE NOTES			**USED CONDITION**
Silver Certificate	1886	Gen. Hancock	25.00
"	1891	William Windom	26.00
"	1896	Fulton and Morse (on Rev.)	90.00
"	1899	Washington	25.00
Treasury or Coin Note	1890	Gen. McPherson	35.00
"	1891	Gen. McPherson	20.00
National Bank Note	Old (original)	Large, horizontal "lazy" 2	125.00
"	1875	Large, horizontal "lazy" 2	125.00
Federal Reserve Bank Note	1918	Jefferson	15.00
SMALL SIZE NOTES			**NEW CONDITION**
U.S. Note	1928 (A-G)	Jefferson	6.00
"	1953 (A-C)	Jefferson	2.50
"	1963 (A)	Jefferson	2.25
Federal Reserve Note	1976	Jefferson	2.00

5 DOLLAR NOTES

Torn, frayed or excessively worn notes command little or no premium.
All modern Federal Reserve Notes after 1974 have no premium.

Type of Issue	Series	Portrait or Main Design	Value
LARGE SIZE NOTES			**USED CONDITION**
Demand Note	1861	Hamilton	300.00
U.S. Note (Legal Tender)	1862	Hamilton	35.00
"	1863	Hamilton	35.00
"	1869	Jackson	32.50
"	1875	Jackson	27.50
"	1878	Jackson	25.00
"	1880	Jackson	20.00
"	1907	Jackson	20.00
Silver Certificate	1886	Grant	150.00
"	1891	Grant	50.00
"	1896	Grant and Sheridan (on Rev.)	160.00
"	1899	Indian Chief, Onepapa	75.00
"	1923	Lincoln	75.00
Treasury or Coin Note	1890	Gen. Thomas	32.00
"		Gen. Thomas	30.00
National Bank Note	Old (original)	Landing of Columbus (on Rev.)	60.00
"	1875	Landing of Columbus (on Rev.)	60.00
"	1882	Garfield; brown back	30.00
"	1882	Garfield; "1882-1908" on back	35.00
"	1882	Garfield; "Five Dollars" on back	40.00
"	1902	Harrison; red seal	20.00
"	1902	Harrison; blue seal; "1902-1908" on back	8.00
"	1902	Harrison; blue seal only	7.00
Federal Reserve Bank Note	1915	Lincoln	12.00
"	1918	Lincoln	12.00
Federal Reserve Note	1914	Lincoln; red seal	12.00
"	1914	Lincoln; blue seal	7.00
National Gold Bank Note	1870-74	Gold coins on bank	300.00
SMALL SIZE NOTES			**NEW CONDITION**
U.S. Note	1928 (A-F)	Lincoln	7.50
"	1953 (A-C)	Lincoln	8.00
"	1963	Lincoln	5.50
Silver Certificate	1934 (A-D)	Lincoln	6.00
"	1953 (A-B)	Lincoln	5.50

Type of Issue	Series	Portrait or Main Design	Value
National Bank Note	1929	Lincoln	**15.00**
Federal Reserve Bank Note	1929	Lincoln	**12.00**
Federal Reserve Note	1928 (A-D)	Lincoln	**8.00**
"	1934 (A-D)	Lincoln	**5.25**
"	1950 (A-E)	Lincoln	**6.00**
"	1963 (A)	Lincoln	**6.00**
"	1969 (A-C)	Lincoln	**6.00**
"	1974 & later	Lincoln	**Current**
Hawaiian Issue (Brown Seal)	1934 (A)	Lincoln	**25.00**
Armed Forces Issue (Yellow Seal)	1934-A	Lincoln	**22.50**

10 DOLLAR NOTES

Torn, frayed or excessively worn notes command little or no premium.
All modern Federal Reserve Notes after 1974 have no premium.

Type of Issue	Series	Portrait or Main Design	Value
LARGE SIZE NOTES			**USED CONDITION**
Demand Note	1861	Lincoln	**350.00**
U.S. Note (Legal Tender)	1862	Lincoln	**50.00**
"	1863	Lincoln	**50.00**
"	1869	Webster	**55.00**
"	1875	Webster	**35.00**
U.S. Note (Legal Tender)	1878	Webster	**35.00**
"	1880	Webster	**27.50**
"	1901	Lewis and Clark; bison	**80.00**
"	1923	Jackson	**150.00**
Compound Interest Note	1863–65	Chase	**175.00**
Interest Bearing Note (one year)	1864	Chase	**375.00**
Refunding Certificate	1879	Franklin	**140.00**
Silver Certificate	1878	Robert Morris	**500.00**
"	1880	Robert Morris	**90.00**
"	1886	Thomas Hendricks	**75.00**
"	1891	Thomas Hendricks	**27.50**
"	1908	Thomas Hendricks	**25.00**
Treasury or Coin Note	1890	Gen. Sheridan	**50.00**
"	1891	Gen. Sheridan	**30.00**
National Bank Note	Old (original)	De Soto at the Mississippi (on Rev.)	**50.00**
"	1875	De Soto at the Mississippi (on Rev.)	**50.00**
"	1882	Franklin with kite: brown back	**25.00**
"	1882	Same with "1882–1908" on back	**25.00**
"	1882	Same with "Ten Dollars" on back	**60.00**
"	1902	McKinley; red seal	**35.00**
"	1902	McKinley; blue seal: "1902–1908" on back	**12.00**
"	1902	McKinley; blue seal only	**12.00**

LARGE SIZE NOTES			**USED CONDITION**
Federal Reserve Bank Note	1915	Jackson	**22.50**
"	1918	Jackson	**22.50**
Federal Reserve Note	1914	Jackson; red seal	**15.00**
"	1914	Jackson; blue seal	**11.00**
National Gold Bank Note	1870–75	Gold coins on back	**325.00**
Gold Certificate	1907	Michael Hillegas	**15.00**
"	1922	Michael Hillegas	**14.00**

Type of Issue	Series	Portrait or Main Design	Value
SMALL SIZE NOTES			**NEW CONDITION**
Silver Certificate	1933	Hamilton	1,200.00
"	1934 (A-D)	Hamilton	12.00
"	1953 (A-B)	Hamilton	11.00
National Bank Note	1929	Hamilton	20.00
Federal Reserve Bank Note	1929	Hamilton	13.00
Federal Reserve Note	1928 (A-C)	Hamilton	11.00
"	1934 (A-D)	Hamilton	11.00
"	1950 (A-E)	Hamilton	11.00
"	1963 (A)	Hamilton	11.00
"	1969 (A-C)	Hamilton	11.00
"	1974 & later	Hamilton	Current
Hawaiian Issue (Brown Seal)	1934-A	Hamilton	35.00
Armed Forces Issue (Yellow Seal)	1934 (A)	Hamilton	30.00
Gold Certificate	1928	Hamilton	45.00

20 DOLLAR NOTES

Torn, frayed or excessively worn notes command little or no premium.
All modern Federal Reserve Notes after 1974 have no premium.

Type of Issue	Series	Portrait or Main Design	Value
LARGE SIZE NOTES			**USED CONDITION**
Demand Note	1861	Liberty Standing	1,200.00
U.S. Note (Legal Tender)	1862	Liberty Standing	50.00
"	1863	Liberty Standing	50.00
"	1869	Hamilton	100.00
"	1875	Hamilton	35.00
"	1878	Hamilton	30.00
"	1880	Hamilton	25.00
Compound Interest Note	1863–65	Lincoln	500.00
Interest Bearing Note (one year)	1864	Lincoln	750.00
Silver Certificate	1878	Stephen Decatur	600.00
"	1880	Stephen Decatur	175.00
"	1886	Daniel Manning	150.00
"	1891	Daniel Manning	40.00
Treasury or Coin Note	1890	John Marshall	125.00
"	1891	John Marshall	125.00
National Bank Note	Old (original)	Baptism of Pocahontas (on Rev.)	75.00
"	1875	Baptism of Pocahontas (on Rev.)	75.00
"	1882	Battle of Lexington; brown back	40.00
"	1882	Same with "1882–1908" on back	45.00
"	1882	Same with "Twenty Dollars" on back	85.00
"	1902	Hugh McCulloch; red seal	30.00
"	1902	Hugh McCulloch; blue seal; "1902–1908" on back	23.00

LARGE SIZE NOTES			**USED CONDITION**
National Bank Note	1902	Hugh McCulloch; blue seal only	22.00
Federal Reserve Bank Note	1915	Cleveland	40.00
"	1918	Cleveland	40.00
Federal Reserve Note	1914	Cleveland; red seal	25.00
"	1914	Cleveland; blue seal	22.00
National Gold Bank Note	1870–75	Gold coins on back	400.00
Gold Certificate	1863	Eagle on shield	—
"	1882	Garfield	32.00
"	1905	Washington	70.00
"	1906	Washington	30.00
"	1922	Washington	27.00

Type of Issue	Series	Portrait or Main Design	Value
SMALL SIZE NOTES			**NEW CONDITION**
National Bank Note	1929	Jackson	**30.00**
Federal Reserve Bank Note	1929	Jackson	**24.00**
Federal Reserve Note	1928 (A-C)	Jackson	**22.50**
"	1934 (A-D)	Jackson	**21.00**
"	1950 (A-E)	Jackson	**20.00**
"	1963 (A)	Jackson	**20.00**
"	1969 (A-C)	Jackson	**20.00**
"	1974 & later	Jackson	**Current**
Hawaiian Issue (Brown Seal)	1934 (A)	Jackson	**50.00**
Gold Certificate	1928	Jackson	**50.00**

50 DOLLAR NOTES

Torn, frayed or excessively worn notes command little or no premium.
All modern Federal Reserve Notes after 1974 have no premium.

Type of Issue	Series	Portrait or Main Design	Value
LARGE SIZE NOTES			**USED CONDITION**
U.S. Note (Legal Tender)	1862	Hamilton	**400.00**
"	1863	Hamilton	**400.00**
"	1869	Henry Clay	**700.00**
"	1874	Franklin	**165.00**
"	1875	Franklin	**150.00**
"	1878	Franklin	**150.00**
"	1880	Franklin	**70.00**
Compound Interest Note	1863–65	Hamilton	**Rare**
Interest Bearing Note (one year)	1864	Hamilton	**Rare**
Interest Bearing Note (two years)	1863	Three females	**Rare**
Interest Bearing Note (three years)	1861	Large eagle	**Rare**
"	1864	Large eagle	**Rare**
"	1865	Large eagle	**Rare**
"	1865	Large eagle	**Rare**
Silver Certificate	1878	Edward Everett	**650.00**
"	1880	Edward Everett	**700.00**
"	1891	Edward Everett	**85.00**
Treasury or Coin Note	1891	William Seward	**1,200.00**
National Bank Note	Old (original)	Embarkation of the Pilgrims (on Rev.)	**450.00**
"	1875	Embarkation of the Pilgrims (on Rev.)	**450.00**
"	1882	Washington Crossing the Delaware and at prayer; brown back	**75.00**
"	1882	Same with "1882–1908" on back	**75.00**
SMALL SIZE NOTES			**USED CONDITION**
Federal Reserve Bank Note	1929	Grant	**51.00**
Federal Reserve Note	1928 (A)	Grant	**50.00**
"	1934 (A-D)	Grant	**50.00**
"	1950 (A-E)	Grant	**50.00**
"	1963-A	Grant	**50.00**
"	1969 (A-C)	Grant	**50.00**
"	1974 & later	Grant	**Current**
Gold Certificate	1928	Grant	**150.00**

100 DOLLAR NOTES

Torn, frayed or excessively worn notes command little or no premium.
All modern Federal Reserve Notes after 1974 have no premium.

Type of Issue	Series	Portrait or Main Design	Value
LARGE SIZE NOTES			**USED CONDITION**
U.S. Note (Legal Tender)	1862	Large eagle	700.00
"	1863	Large eagle	700.00
"	1869	Lincoln	1,000.00
"	1875	Lincoln	650.00
"	1878	Lincoln	650.00
"	1880	Lincoln	175.00
Compound Interest Note	1863–65	Washington standing	700.00
Interest Bearing Note (one year)	1864	Washington standing	Rare
Interest Bearing Note (two years)	1863	Agriculture and Industry	Rare
Interest Bearing Note (three years)	1861	Gen. Scott	Rare
"	1865	Gen. Scott	Rare
Silver Certificate	1878	Monroe	800.00
"	1880	Monroe	700.00
"	1891	Monroe	325.00
Treasury or Coin Note	1890	Commodore Farragut	1,000.00
"	1891	Commodore Farragut	1,000.00
National Bank Note	Old (original)	Signing of the Declaration of Independence (on Rev.)	500.00
"	1875	Signing the Declaration of Independence (on Rev.)	500.00
"	1882	Commodore Perry leaving his flagship; brown back	125.00
"	1882	Same with "1882–1908" on back	120.00
"	1882	Same with "One Hundred Dollars" on back	Rare
"	1902	John Knox; red seal	110.00
"	1902	John Knox; blue seal; "1902–1908" on back	100.00
"	1902	John Knox; blue seal only	100.00
Federal Reserve Note	1914	Franklin; red seal	100.00
"	1914	Franklin; blue seal	100.00
National Gold Bank Note	1870–75	Gold coins on back	2,000.00
Gold certificate	1863	Eagle on shield	——
"	1870–71	Thomas Benton	——
"	1875	Thomas Benton	
"	1882	Thomas Benton	110.00
"	1922	Thomas Benton	125.00
SMALL SIZE NOTES			**NEW CONDITION**
National Bank Note	1929	Franklin	115.00
Federal Reserve Bank Note	1929	Franklin	110.00
Federal Reserve Note	1928 (A)	Franklin	105.00
"	1934 (A-D)	Franklin	100.00
"	1950 (A-E)	Franklin	100.00
"	1963-A	Franklin	100.00
"	1969 (A-C)	Franklin	100.00
"	1974 & later	Franklin	Current
U.S. Note (Legal Tender)	1966 (A)	Franklin	200.00
Gold Certificate	1928	Franklin	150.00

FRACTIONAL CURRENCY

Torn, frayed or excessively worn notes command little or no premium.

3 Cent Notes

Years of Issue	Description	Used
1864–1869	Small head of Washington.	3.00

5 Cent Notes

Years of Issue	Description	Used
1862–1863	Facsimile of a 5 Cent postage stamp with head of Jefferson.	2.00
1862–1863	Same as above but with perforated edges.	2.50
1863–1867	Head of Washington in bronze oval frame. Brown back.	1.50
1864–1869	Head of Spencer M. Clark. Green back.	1.50
1864–1869	Same as above but with red back.	2.00

10 Cent Notes

Years of Issue	Description	Used
1862–1863	Facsimile of a 10 Cent postage stamp with head of Washington.	2.00
1862–1863	Same as above but with perforated edges.	2.50
1863–1867	Head of Washington in bronze oval frame. Green back.	1.50
1864–1869	Head of Washington. A bronze "1O" in each corner. Green back.	1.50
1864–1869	Same as above but with red back.	2.50
1869–1875	Bust of Liberty.	1.25
1874–1876	Head of William M. Meredith. Green seal.	1.25
1874–1876	Same as above but with red seal.	1.00

15 Cent Notes

Years of Issue	Description	Used
1869–1875	Bust of Columbia.	3.50
Not Issued	Heads of Grant and Sherman. Separate front and back. Green back.	20.00
Not Issued	Same as above but with red back.	20.00

25 Cent Notes

Years of Issue	Description	Used
1862–1863	Facsimiles of five 5 Cent postage stamps with head of Jefferson.	3.00
1862–1863	Same as above but with perforated edges.	4.00
1863–1867	Head of Washington in bronze oval frame. Purple back.	1.75
1864–1869	Bust of Fessenden. Green back.	1.75
1864–1869	Same as above but with red back.	3.00
1869–1875	Bust of Washington.	1.25
1874–1876	Bust of Robert V. Walker.	.75

50 Cent Notes

Years of Issue	Description	Used
1862–1863	Facsimiles of five 10 Cent postage stamps with head of Washington.	3.00
1862–1863	Same as above but with perforated edges.	5.00
1863–1867	Head of Washington in bronze oval frame. Red back.	1.75
1864–1869	Bust of Gen. Spinner. Green back with a "50" at each end.	1.75
1864–1869	Same as above but with red back.	2.00
1864–1869	Bust of Gen. Spinner. Green back with "50" in center.	1.75
1864–1869	Seated figure of Justice. Green back.	2.00
1864–1869	Same as above but with red back.	2.00
1869–1875	Bust of Lincoln.	4.00
1869–1875	Bust of E. M. Stanton.	2.00
1869–1875	Bust of Samuel Dexter.	2.50
1874–1876	Bust of William Crawford.	1.50

Confederate States of America

Torn, frayed or excessively worn notes command little or no premium.

PAPER MONEY ISSUES

All notes were issued from Richmond, Virginia, except the few 1861 issues listed as from Montgomery, Alabama.

In recent years, facsimiles have been made of many Confederate notes. Many people mistake them for genuine pieces. They are usually on much heavier paper and are invariably in new condition. In many cases, the word, "Facsimile," may actually be found in quite small letters somewhere on the note.

Confederate notes will sometimes be found cut or slit in a regular pattern, or with holes punched through. These indicate cancellation by the Confederacy, and are worth less than uncancelled specimens.

For further general comment on Confederate currency, please see under "United States Paper Money" in the General Information following the Preface.

50 CENT NOTES

Years of Issue	Portrait or Main Design	Used
1863	Jefferson Davis. Blank Rev.	1.25
1864	Similar to above except for date.	1.00

1 DOLLAR NOTES

Years of Issue	Portrait or Main Design	Used
1862	Steamship with sails; female standing at left; Lucy Pickens at right. Blank Rev.	4.00
1862	Similar to above, but overprinted with a large green "1" and "ONE." Blank Rev.	6.00
1862	C. Clay. Blank Rev.	4.00
1863	Similar to above except for date.	3.25
1864	Similar to above except for date.	1.00

2 DOLLAR NOTES

Years of Issue	Portrait or Main Design	Used
1861	The "South" attacking the "North" with sword; J. P. Benjamin at left. Blank Rev.	· 25.00
1862	The "South" attacking the "North" with sword; J. P. Benjamin at left. Blank Rev.	10.00
1862	Similar to above but overprinted with a large green "2" and "TWO." Blank Rev.	15.00
1862	Ornamented "2" in center; J. P. Benjamin at right. Blank Rev.	5.00
1863	Similar to above except for date.	5.00
1864	Similar to above except for date.	4.00

5 DOLLAR NOTES

Years of Issue	Portrait or Main Design	Used
1861	Liberty seated with shield and eagle, a "5" in front; sailor at left. Blank Rev.	225.00
1861	"V" in upper left; "5" in upper right. Blue Rev.	200.00
1861	Five females seated; standing female at left; Washington at right. Blank Rev.	27.50
1861	Child at left; blacksmith at right. Blank Rev.	30.00
1861	C. Memminger; Minerva at right, "V" below. Blank Rev.	13.00
1861	Similar to above except that "FIVE" is below Minerva. Blank Rev.	5.00
1861	Blacks loading cotton on ship at left: indian girl at right. Blank Rev.	275.00
1861	Female seated on cotton bale, sailor at left. Blank Rev.	3.00
1861	Sailor and cotton bales; C. Memminger at left; two females at right. Blank Rev.	4.00
1862	State Capitol at Richmond, Va.: C. Memminger at right. Blue Rev.	3.00
1863	Similar to above except for date.	3.00
1864	Similar to above except for date.	2.00

10 DOLLAR NOTES

Years of Issue	Portrait or Main Design	Used
1861	Liberty seated with shield and eagle; female at left. Blank Rev.	3.00
1861	Indian family; female with trident at left; female with "X" at right. Blank Rev.	32.50
1861	Cotton wagon; male bust at left; harvester at right. Blank Rev.	35.00
1861	R. Hunter at left; a child at right. Blank Rev.	12.00
1861	Female with anchor; R. Hunter at left; C. Memminger at right. Blank Rev.	5.00
1861	Similar to above except that an "X" is overprinted in red at each side of the female. Blank Rev.	5.00
	Liberty with eagle and shield at upper left; small train at right. Blank Rev.	250.00
1861	Two females with urn at upper left; small train at right. Blank Rev.	3.00
1861	Black with cotton; landscape at right. Blank Rev.	8.00
1861	Military figures at dinner; R. Hunter at left; Minerva at right. Blank Rev.	5.00
1861	Female leaning on cotton bales, ships in rear; R. Hunter at right. Blank Rev.	5.00
1862	Female seated with wheat; R. Hunter at right. Blank Rev.	600.00
1862	State Capitol at Columbia, S. C.; R. Hunter at right. Blue Rev.	2.00
1862	Similar to above except for date.	2.00
1863	Horses pulling artillery pieces; R. Hunter at right. Blue Rev.	2.00
1864		

20 DOLLAR NOTES

Years of Issue	Portrait or Main Design	Used
1861	Full masted sailing ship. Blank Rev.	5.00
1861	Three females in center, Liberty standing at left. Blank Rev.	60.00
1861	Full masted sailing ship; sailor at left. Blank Rev.	3.00
1861	Female with globe; female at left; blacksmith at right. Blank Rev.	200.00
1861	Female between Cupid and beehive; Vice President Stephens at left; female with anchor at right. Blank Rev.	4.00
1861	Vice-President Stephens. Blank Rev.	17.50
1862	Liberty seated with shield of the Confederacy; R. Hunter at right. Blank Rev.	450.00
1862	State Capitol at Nashville, Tenn.; Stephens at right. Blue Rev.	4.00
1863	Similar to above except for date.	2.00
1864	Similar to above except for date.	2.00

50 DOLLAR NOTES

Years of Issue	Portrait or Main Design	Used
1861	Three black farm workers. Blank Rev. Montgomery, Ala.	700.00
1861	Two females on cotton bale; Justice at left; Washington at right. Blank Rev.	60.00
1861	Washington in center; seated figure at left. Blank Rev.	8.00
1861	Female and money chests; two sailors at left. Blank Rev.	6.00
1861	Railroad train; female with anchor at left; female with scales at right. Blank Rev.	225.00
1861	Jefferson Davis. Blank Rev.	8.00
1862	Jefferson Davis. Green Rev.	7.50
1863	Similar to above except for date.	7.50
1864	Similar to above except for date and a Blue Rev.	3.50

100 DOLLAR NOTES

Years of Issue	Portrait or Main Design	Used
1861	Railroad train in center; Liberty at left. Blank Rev. Montgomery, Ala.	800.00
1861	Railroad train in center; Justice at left; Minerva at right. Blank Rev.	65.00
1861	Two females in cloud; Washington at left. Blank Rev.	50.00
1861	Blacks loading cotton wagon; sailor at left. Blank Rev.	10.00
1862	Railroad train; miikmaid at left. Blank Rev.	6.00
1862	Blacks in cotton field; J. C. Calhoun at left; Liberty at right. Blank Rev.	10.00
1862	Lucy Pickens; two soldiers at left; Randolph at right. Green Rev.	24.00
1863	Similar to above except for date.	7.00
1864	Similar to above except for date and a Blue Rev.	5.00

500 DOLLAR NOTES

Years of Issue	Portrait or Main Design	Used
1861	Train on bridge; cattle below. Blank Rev. Montgomery, Ala.	2,000.00
1864	Confederate flag over horseman at left; "Stonewall" Jackson at right. Blank Rev.	50.00

1,000 DOLLAR NOTE

Years of Issue	Portrait or Main Design	Used
1861	John C. Calhoun and Andrew Jackson. Blank Rev. Montgomery, Ala.	2,400.00

CONFEDERATE COIN ISSUES

No Confederate coin was ever struck for actual circulation. However, four genuine trial specimens of a half dollar were allegedly struck. The reverse die of this coin was used at a later date to manufacture restrikes and it is these restrikes which appear on the market. Genuine U.S. half dollars of 1861 were used for this purpose, the reverse being planed off and then struck with the Confederate die.

The so-called Confederate Cent of 1861 shows a Liberty Head on the Obv. and the value on the Rev. A few specimens were struck privately in Philadelphia at the instigation of the Confederacy, but no coins were ever delivered. Both restrikes and modern replicas exist of this coin.

Denomination	Year	Amount Minted	Value
CONFEDERATE SILVER HALF DOLLAR.	1861	Fine	500.00
CONFEDERATE COPPER CENT.	1861	Proof	1,250.00

The Coinage of British North America
CANADA

LARGE CENTS
Head of Queen Victoria

Date	Amount Minted	Value	Date	Amount Minted	Value
1858	421,000	15.00	1892	1¼ million	.40
1859	9½ million	.50	1893	2 million	.30
1876-H	4 million	.50	1894	1 million	1.00
1881-H	2 million	.75	1895	1¼ million	.60
1882-H	4 million	.30	1896	2 million	.40
1884	2½ million	.30	1897	1½ million	.40
1886	1½ million	.65	1898-H	1 million	1.25
1887	1½ million	.50	1899	2½ million	.40
1888	4 million	.30	1900	1 million	1.50
1890-H	1 million	1.50	1900-H	2⅔ million	.30
1891 Large date	1½ million	1.50	1901	4 million	.30
1891 Small date	Part of above	15.00			

Head of King Edward VII

Date	Amount Minted	Value	Date	Amount Minted	Value
1902	3 million	.25	1907	2½ million	.25
1903	4 million	.25	1907-H	800,000	2.50
1904	2½ million	.30	1908	2½ million	.25
1905	2 million	.40	1909	4 million	.20
1906	4 million	.25	1910	5 million	.20

Head of King George V

Date	Amount Minted	Value	Date	Amount Minted	Value
1911	4⅔ million	.15	1916	11 million	.10
1912	5 million	.15	1917	12 million	.10
1913	5¾ million	.15	1918	13 million	.10
1914	3½ million	.25	1919	11¼ million	.10
1915	4¾ million	.15	1920	7 million	.10

SMALL CENTS
Head of King George V

Date	Amount Minted	Value	Date	Amount Minted	Value
1920	15½ million	.04	1929	12¼ million	.03
1921	7½ million	.05	1930	2½ million	.40
1922	1¼ million	3.00	1931	3¾ million	.20
1923	1 million	6.00	1932	21½ million	.02
1924	1½ million	1.00	1933	12 million	.02
1925	1 million	3.50	1934	7 million	.05
1926	2¼ million	.50	1935	7½ million	.05
1927	3½ million	.25	1936	8¾ million	.05
1928	9 million	.03			

Head of King George VI

(The following valuations are for coins in brilliant, new condition, and showing no signs of wear. Used or circulated Cents from 1937 to date do not command a premium.)

Date	Amount Minted	Value	Date	Amount Minted	Value
1937	10 million	.50	1946	56²/₃ million	.10
1938	18¹/₂ million	.50	1947	31 million	.50
1939	21²/₃ million	.50	1947 Maple leaf	43³/₄ million	.35
1940	85³/₄ million	.25	1948	24³/₄ million	.50
1941	56¹/₂ million	2.50	1949	33¹/₂ million	.25
1942	76 million	2.00	1950	60¹/₂ million	.25
1943	89 million	1.00	1951	80¹/₂ million	.10
1944	44¹/₄ million	2.00	1952	67²/₃ million	.10
1945	77¹/₂ million	.10			

Obv. Type 1953–1964	Rev. Type 1937–	Obv. Type 1965–	Commemorative Rev. 1967

Head of Queen Elizabeth II

(The valuations are for coins in brilliant, new condition)

Date	Amount Minted	Value	Date	Amount Minted	Value
1953	72¹/₄ million	.05	1975	642¹/₂ million	.01
1954	22 million	.10	1976	701 million	.01
1955	56²/₃ million	.05	1977	453 million	.01
1956	78²/₃ million	.05	1978	911 million	.01
1957	100¹/₂ million	.05	1979	754 million	.01
1958	57³/₄ million	.05	1980	911³/₄ million	.01
1959	83²/₃ million	.05	1982	876 million	.01
1960	75³/₄ million	.05	1983	975¹/₂ million	.01
1961	139¹/₂ million	.05	1984	838¹/₄ million	.01
1962	227¹/₄ million	.05	1985	126.6 million	.01
1963	279 million	.05	1986	740.3 million	.01
1964	484²/₃ million	.05	1987	774.5 million	.01
1965	304¹/₂ million	.01	1988	482.7 million	.01
1966	183²/₃ million	.01	1989	1.1 billion	.01
1967	345¹/₄ million	.01	1990	205.4 million	.01
1968	329²/₃ million	.01	1991		.01
1969	335¹/₄ million	.01	1992		.01
1970	311¹/₄ million	.01	1993		.01
1971	298¹/₄ million	.01	1994		.01
1972	451¹/₃ million	.01			
1973	457 million	.01			
1974	692 million	.01			

SILVER 5 CENTS

Head of Queen Victoria

(The following valuations are for coins in G-VG condition)

Date	Amount Minted	Value	Date	Amount Minted	Value
1858 Small date	1½ million	2.50	1887	500,000	3.00
1858 Large date	Part of above	23.00	1888	1 million	1.10
1870	2¾ million	2.50	1889	1¼ million	4.00
1871	1½ million	2.50	1890-H	1 million	1.00
1872-H	2 million	1.00	1891	1¾ million	1.10
1874-H	800,000	2.50	1892	860,000	1.25
1875-H	1 million	20.00	1893	1¾ million	1.00
1880-H	3 million	.75	1894	500,000	2.00
1881-H	1½ million	1.00	1896	1½ million	1.00
1882-H	1 million	1.00	1897	1½ million	1.00
1883-H	600,000	2.50	1898	580,717	1.50
1884	200,000	20.00	1899	3 million	.35
1885	1 million	1.50	1900	1¾ million	.35
1886	1¾ million	1.10	1901	2 million	.35

Head of King Edward VII

Date	Amount Minted	Value	Date	Amount Minted	Value
1902	2 million	.50	1906	3 million	.40
1902-H	2¼ million	.50	1907	1¼ million	.40
1903	1 million	1.00	1908	1¼ million	1.00
1903-H	2⅔ million	.60	1909	1¾ million	.75
1904	2½ million	.50	1910	6 million	.40
1905	2⅔ million	.50			

Head of King George V

Date	Amount Minted	Value	Date	Amount Minted	Value
1911	3⅔ million	.40	1917	5⅔ million	.25
1912	5¾ million	.25	1918	5¾ million	.25
1913	5½ million	.25	1919	8 million	.25
1914	4¼ million	.25	1920	10⅔ million	.25
1915	1¼ million	2.00	1921	2½ million	1,000.00
1916	2⅓ million	.50			

NICKEL 5 CENTS

Head of King George V

Date	Amount Minted	Value	Date	Amount Minted	Value
1922	4³/₄ million	.06	1930	3²/₃ million	.07
1923	2¹/₂ million	.07	1931	5 million	.06
1924	3 million	.06	1932	3¹/₄ million	.07
1925	200,050	10.00	1933	2¹/₂ million	.07
1926	933,577	1.00	1934	3³/₄ million	.06
1927	5¹/₄ million	.06	1935	3³/₄ million	.06
1928	4¹/₂ million	.06	1936	4¹/₂ million	.06
1929	5¹/₂ million	.06			

Beaver Type	V for Victory	Nickel
1937–1942 & 1946–1952	1943–1945	Bicentennial
		1951

Head of King George VI
Beginning with the 1942 Tombac issue, the shape of the nickel is 12-sided, rather than round

Date	Amount Minted	Value	Date	Amount Minted	Value
1937	5 million	.10	1946	7 million	.05
1938	4 million	.25	1947	7²/₃ million	.05
1939	5²/₃ million	.05	1947 Maple Leaf	9¹/₂ million	.05
1940	14 million	.05	1948	1³/₄ million	.15
1941	8²/₃ million	.05	1949	13 million	.05
1942-Nickel	6³/₄ million	.05	1950	12 million	.05
1942 Tombac	3¹/₂ million	.08	1951 Regular	4¹/₂ million	.08
1943	24³/₄ million	.05	1951 Commem.	9 million	.05
1944	11¹/₂ million	.05	1952	10³/₄ million	.05
1945	18³/₄ million	.05			

12-sided 1953–1962   *Mature Head Type*   *Commemorative*
Round 1963–1964   *1965–*   *Rev. 1967*

Head of Queen Elizabeth II

Date	Amount Minted	Value	Date	Amount Minted	Value
1953	16²/₃ million	.05	1975	138.8 million	.05
1954	7 million	.05	1976	55 million	.05
1955	5¹/₂ million	.05	1977	89 million	.05
1956	9¹/₂ million	.05	1978	137 million	.05
1957	7¹/₂ million	.05	1979	186¹/₄ million	.05
1958	7¹/₂ million	.05	1980	134³/₄ million	.05
1959	11¹/₂ million	.05	1981	99 million	.05
1960	37 million	.05	1982	105¹/₂ million	.05
1961	47³/₄ million	.05	1983	72¹/₂ million	.05
1962	46¹/₄ million	.05	1984	84 million	.05
1963	44 million	.05	1985	126.6 million	.05
1964	78 million	.05	1986	156.1 million	.05
1965	84³/₄ million	.05	1987	106.3 million	.05
1966	27¹/₂ million	.05	1988	75 million	.05
1967	58³/₄ million	.05	1989	141.4 million	.05
1968	99¹/₄ million	.05	1990	42.4 million	.05
1969	27³/₄ million	.05	1991		.05
1970	5³/₄ million	.05	1992		.05
1971	27¹/₂ million	.05	1993		.05
1972	62¹/₂ million	.05	1994		.05
1973	53¹/₂ million	.05			
1974	94³/₄ million	.05			

10 CENTS

Head of Queen Victoria

Date	Amount Minted	Value	Date	Amount Minted	Value
1858	1¼ million	3.00	1888	500,000	3.00
1870	1⅔ million	3.00	1889	600,000	100.00
1871	800,000	3.00	1890-H	450,000	2.75
1871-H	1¾ million	4.00	1891	800,000	2.75
1872-H	1 million	15.00	1892	520,000	2.25
1874-H	600,000	2.25	1893 Flat top 3	500,000	3.00
1875-H	1 million	60.00	1893 Round top 3	Part of above	175.00
1880-H	1½ million	2.25	1894	500,000	1.75
1881-H	950,000	2.00	1896	650,000	1.25
1882-H	1 million	1.75	1898	720,000	1.25
1883-H	300,000	4.50	1899	1¼ million	.75
1884	150,000	40.00	1900	1 million	.40
1885	400,000	3.25	1901	1¼ million	.40
1886	800,000	2.50			
1887	350,000	2.75			

Head of King Edward VII

Date	Amount Minted	Value	Date	Amount Minted	Value
1902	720,000	.50	1906	1⅓ million	.35
1902-H	1 million	.50	1907	2⅔ million	.35
1903	500,000	.75	1908	761,631	.50
1903-H	1½ million	.35	1909	1½ million	.35
1904	1 million	.50	1910	4⅔ million	.35
1905	1 million	.40			

Head of King George V

Date	Amount Minted	Value	Date	Amount Minted	Value
1911	2³/₄ million	**2.00**	1921	2¹/₂ million	**.50**
1912	3¹/₄ million	**.25**	1928	2¹/₂ million	**.20**
1913 Small leaves	3¹/₂ million	**.25**	1929	3¹/₄ million	**.20**
1913 Large leaves	Part of above	**20.00**	1930	1³/₄ million	**.20**
1914	2¹/₂ million	**.40**	1931	2 million	**.20**
1915	672,408	**.75**	1932	1¹/₄ million	**.30**
1916	4¹/₄ million	**.25**	1933	672,368	**.35**
1917	5 million	**.25**	1934	384,056	**.25**
1918	5 million	**.25**	1935	384,592	**.25**
1919	7³/₄ million	**.25**	1936	2³/₄ million	**.25**
1920	6¹/₄ million	**.25**			

Head of King George VI

Date	Amount Minted	Value	Date	Amount Minted	Value
1937	2¹/₂ million	**.30**	1946	6¹/₃ million	**.20**
1938	4¹/₄ million	**.35**	1947	4¹/₂ million	**.20**
1939	5¹/₂ million	**.20**	1947 Maple leaf	9²/₃ million	**.20**
1940	16¹/₂ million	**.20**	1948	422,7411	**1.50**
1941	8³/₄ million	**.20**	1949	11¹/₂ million	**.20**
1942	10¹/₄ million	**.20**	1950	17³/₄ million	**.20**
1943	21¹/₄ million	**.20**	1951	15 million	**.20**
1944	9¹/₂ million	**.20**	1952	10¹/₂ million	**.20**
1945	11 million	**.20**			

Obv. Type	Rev. Type	Obv. Type	Commemorative
1953–1964	1937–	1965–	Rev. 1967

Head of Queen Elizabeth II

Date	Amount Minted	Value	Date	Amount Minted	Value
1953	18½ million	.15	1975	207⅔ million	.10
1954	4½ million	.15	1976	95 million	.10
1955	12¼ million	.15	1977	128½ million	.10
1956	16¾ million	.15	1978	170½ million	.10
1957	15⅔ million	.15	1979	237 million	.10
1958	11 million	.15	1980	169¾ million	.10
1959	19⅔ million	.15	1981	124 million	.10
1960	45½ million	.15	1982	94 million	.10
1961	26¾ million	.15	1983	111 million	.10
1962	41¾ million	.15	1984	119 million	.10
1963	42 million	.15	1985	143 million	.10
1964	49½ million	.15	1986	168.6 million	.10
1965	57 million	.15	1987	147.3 million	.10
1966	34½ million	.15	1988	163 million	.10
1967	63 million	.15	1989	198.7 million	.10
1968 Silver	70½ million	.15	1990	64.4 million	.10
1968 Nickel	107 million	.10	1991		.10
1969	55¾ million	.10	1992		.10
1970	5¼ million	.10	1993		.10
1971	41 million	.10	1994		.10
1972	60 million	.10			
1973	167¾ million	.10			
1974	201½ million	.10			

20 CENTS

Head of Queen Victoria

Date	Amount Minted	Value
1858	750,000	15.00

25 CENTS

Head of Queen Victoria

Date	Amount Minted	Value	Date	Amount Minted	Value
1870	900,000	3.75	1887	100,000	20.00
1871	400,000	4.50	1888	400,000	2.75
1871-H	748,000	5.00	1889	66,340	75.00
1872-H	2¼ million	2.50	1890-H	200,000	3.25
1874-H	1²/₃ million	2.50	1891	120,000	12.50
1875-H	1 million	50.00	1892	510,000	2.75
1880-H	400,000	4.25	1893	100,000	15.00
1881-H	820,000	3.50	1894	220,000	3.00
1882-H	600,000	3.75	1899	415,580	1.50
1883-H	960,000	2.50	1900	1¹/₃ million	1.00
1885	192,000	20.00	1901	640,000	1.00
1886	540,000	2.75			

Head of King Edward VII

Date	Amount Minted	Value	Date	Amount Minted	Value
1902	464,000	1.00	1906	1¼ million	1.00
1902-H	800,000	1.00	1907	2 million	1.00
1903	846,150	1.00	1908	466,625	1.50
1904	400,000	3.00	1909	1¹/₃ million	1.00
1905	800,000	1.00	1910	3¹/₂ million	1.00

Head of King George V

Date	Amount Minted	Value	Date	Amount Minted	Value
1911	1²/₃ million	2.50	1927	468,096	7.00
1912	2¹/₂ million	1.00	1928	2 million	.50
1913	2¹/₄ million	1.00	1929	2²/₃ million	.50
1914	1¹/₄ million	1.00	1930	961,174	1.00
1915	238,378	2.00	1931	537,815	1.00
1916	1¹/₂ million	1.00	1932	537,994	1.00
1917	3¹/₄ million	.75	1933	421,282	1.25
1918	4¹/₄ million	.75	1934	384,505	1.25
1919	5³/₄ million	.75	1935	537,997	1.25
1920	2 million	.75	1936	972,094	.75
1921	575,268	2.00	1936 Dot below date	153,685	10.00

Head of King George VI

Date	Amount Minted	Value	Date	Amount Minted	Value
1937	2²/₃ million	.40	1946	2¹/₄ million	.40
1938	3¹/₄ million	.40	1947	1¹/₂ million	.40
1939	3¹/₂ million	.40	1947 Maple leaf	4¹/₃ million	.40
1940	9¹/₂ million	.40	1948	2¹/₂ million	.40
1941	6²/₃ million	.40	1949	8 million	.40
1942	7 million	.40	1950	9²/₃ million	.40
1943	13¹/₂ million	.40	1951	8¹/₄ million	.40
1944	7¹/₄ million	.40	1952	8³/₄ million	.40
1945	5¹/₄ million	.40			

Obv. Type 1953–1964	Rev. Type 1937–	Obv. Type 1965–	Commemorative Rev. 1967	Commemorative Rev. 1973

Head of Queen Elizabeth II

Date	Amount Minted	Value	Date	Amount Minted	Value
1953	11¼ million	.40	1975	141 million	.25
1954	2½ million	.40	1976	86.8 million	.25
1955	9½ million	.40	1977	99⅔ million	.25
1956	11¼ million	.40	1978	176½ million	.25
1957	12⅓ million	.40	1979	131 million	.25
1958	9¾ million	.40	1980	76 million	.25
1959	13½ million	.40	1981	131½ million	.25
1960	22¾ million	.40	1982	131 million	.25
1961	18¼ million	.40	1983	167 million	.25
1962	29½ million	.40	1984	119¼ million	.25
1963	21¼ million	.40	1985	158.7 million	.25
1964	36½ million	.40	1986	132.2 million	.25
1965	44¾ million	.40	1987	53.4 million	.25
1966	25½ million	.40	1988	80.3 million	.25
1967	48¾ million	.40	1989	119.6 million	.25
1968 Silver	71½ million	.40	1990	31.1 million	.25
1968 Nickel	88⅔ million	.25	1991		.25
1969	133 million	.25	1992		.25
1970	10½ million	.25	1993		.25
1971	48 million	.25	1994		.25
1972	43¾ million	.25			
1973	135 million	.25			
1974	192⅓ million	.25			

125th Anniversary of Confederation

The obverse of all coins portrays Queen Elizabeth; the reverses were designed by Canadian citizens from a national competetion for each of the ten provinces and two territories; All coins bear the date "1867–1992"

Province	Metal	Amount Minted	Value
Alberta	Cupro-Nickel	10 million	.50
Alberta	Sterling Silver Proof		4.00
British Columbia	Cupro-Nickel	10 million	.50
British Columbia	Sterling Silver Proof		4.00
Manitoba	Cupro-Nickel	10 million	.50
Manitoba	Sterling Silver Proof		4.00
New Brunswick	Cupro-Nickel	10 million	.50
New Brunswick	Sterling Silver Proof		4.00
Newfoundland	Cupro-Nickel	10 million	.50
Newfoundland	Sterling Silver Proof		4.00
Northwest Territories	Cupro-Nickel	10 million	.50
Northwest Territories	Sterling Silver Proof		4.00
Novia Scotia	Cupro-Nickel	10 million	.50
Novia Scotia	Sterling Silver Proof		4.00
Ontario	Cupro-Nickel	10 million	.50
Ontario	Sterling Silver Proof		4.00
Prince Edward Island	Cupro-Nickel	10 million	.50
Prince Edward Island	Sterling Silver Proof		4.00
Quebec	Cupro-Nickel	10 million	.50
Quebec	Sterling Silver Proof		4.00
Saskatchewan	Cupro-Nickel	10 million	.50
Saskatchewan	Sterling Silver Proof		4.00
Yukon	Cupro-Nickel	10 million	.50
Yukon	Sterling Silver Proof		4.00

50 CENTS

Head of Queen Victoria

Date	Amount Minted	Value	Date	Amount Minted	Value
1870	450,000	**15.00**	1892	151,000	**12.50**
1871	200,000	**20.00**	1894	29,036	**65.00**
1871-H	45,000	**30.00**	1898	100,000	**12.00**
1872-H	80,000	**12.50**	1899	50,000	**32.50**
1881-H	150,000	**12.50**	1900	118,000	**20.00**
1888	60,000	**30.00**	1901	80,000	**10.00**
1890-H	20,000	**250.00**			

Head of King Edward VII

Date	Amount Minted	Value	Date	Amount Minted	Value
1902	120,000	**2.50**	1907	300,000	**2.00**
1903-H	140,000	**4.00**	1908	121,260	**4.00**
1904	60,000	**25.00**	1909	198,648	**3.00**
1905	40,000	**35.00**	1910	640,141	**2.00**
1906	350,000	**2.50**			

The valuations listed in this book closely approximate how much established coin dealers will pay for any material needed in their stock.

Head of King George V

Date	Amount Minted	Value	Date	Amount Minted	Value
1911	204,475	4.00	1920	559,521	2.00
1912	283,248	2.00	1921	176,793	7,000.00
1913	263,290	2.00	1929	228,021	2.00
1914	157,537	20.00	1931	57,581	2.50
1916	454,853	2.00	1932	19,213	15.00
1917	739,715	2.00	1934	38,435	4.00
1918	832,805	2.00	1936	38,550	5.00
1919	1 million	2.00			

Head of King George VI

Date	Amount Minted	Value	Date	Amount Minted	Value
1937	192,016	2.00	1947	424,885	1.00
1938	192,018	2.00	1947 Maple leaf,		
1939	287,976	2.00	straight 7	38,433	·7.00
1940	2 million	.75	1947 Maple leaf,		
1941	1⅔ million	.75	curved 7	Part of above.	650.00
1942	2 million	.75	1948	37,784	17.50
1943	3 million	.75	1949	858,991	2.00
1944	2½ million	.75	1950	2½ million	2.00
1945	2 million	.75	1951	2½ million	.75
1946	950,235	.75	1952	2½ million	.75

**(The valuations in this book are based on the coins
being in G-VG condition, unless otherwise noted.)**

Obv. Type	First Rev. Type	Second Rev. Type	Commem.	Obv. Type
1953–1964	1953–1958	1959–	Rev. 1967	1965–

Head of Queen Elizabeth II

Date	Amount Minted	Value	Date	Amount Minted	Value
1953	1³/₄ million	.75	1975	3³/₄ million	.50
1954	506,305	.75	1976	3 million	.50
1955	753,511	.75	1977	709,939	1.00
1956	1¹/₃ million	.75	1978	3¹/₃ million	.50
1957	2¹/₄ million	.75	1979	3¹/₂ million	.50
1958	3 million	.75	1980	1¹/₂ million	.50
1959	3 million	.75	1981	2³/₄ million	.50
1960	3¹/₂ million	.75	1982	2¹/₃ million	.50
1961	3¹/₂ million	.75	1983	2¹/₄ million	.50
1962	5¹/₄ million	.75	1984	1¹/₄ million	.50
1963	8¹/₃ million	.75	1985	2.2 million	.50
1964	9¹/₂ million	.75	1986	781,400	.50
1965	12²/₃ million	.75	1987	373,000	.50
1966	7²/₃ million	.75	1988	220,000	.50
1967	4¹/₄ million	.75	1989	266,419	.50
1968 Nickel, reduced size,	4 million	.50	1990	207,000	.50
1969	7¹/₂ million	.50	1991		.50
1970	2¹/₂ million	.50	1992		.50
1971	2¹/₄ million	.50	1993		.50
1972	2¹/₂ million	.50	1994		.50
1973	2¹/₂ million	.50			
1974	3¹/₂ million	.50			

SILVER DOLLARS

Commemorative
1935

Regular Issue
1936

Rev. Type
1935–1936

Head of King George V

Date	Amount Minted	Used	Unc	Date	Amount Minted	Used	Unc
1935	428,120	**6.00**	**20.00**	1936	306,100	**4.00**	**20.00**

Obv. Type
1937–1952

Regular Rev.
1937–1952

Commemorative Rev.
1939

Commemorative Rev.
1949

Head of King George VI

Date	Amount Minted	Used	Unc	Date	Amount Minted	Used	Unc
1937	241,002	**3.50**	**15.00**	1947 Maple leaf	21,135	**50.00**	**125.00**
1938	90,304	**10.00**	**35.00**	1948	18,780	**200.00**	**450.00**
1939	1⅓ million	**3.50**	**6.00**	1949	672,298	**10.00**	**14.00**
1945	38,391	**35.00**	**100.00**	1950	261,002	**3.00**	**7.00**
1946	93,055	**7.50**	**35.00**	1951	420,620	**3.50**	**5.00**
1947 Blunt 7	65,595	**15.00**	**50.00**	1952	408,835	**3.50**	**5.00**
1947 Pointed 7	Part of above	**40.00**	**175.00**				

Obv. Type
1953–1964

Regular Rev. Type

Obv. Type
1965–

Commemorative Rev.
1958

Commemorative Rev.
1964

Commemorative Rev.
1967

Commemorative Rev.
1970

Commemorative Rev.
Nickel—1971

Commemorative Rev.
Silver—1971

Commemorative Rev.
Nickel—1973

Commemorative Rev.
Silver–1973

Commemorative Rev.
1974

Commemorative Rev.
Silver—1975

Commemorative Rev.
Silver—1976

Commemorative Rev.
Silver—1977

Note: From 1981 onwards, .500 fine silver dollars exist in both proof-like (Unc) and, only as parts of sets, proof.

Head of Queen Elizabeth II

All Dollars dated 1935 through 1967 were composed of .800 silver

Date	Description	Mintage	Used	Unc
1953	Voyageur	1.1 million	3.00	5.00
1954	Voyageur	246,606	4.00	6.00
1955	Voyageur	268,105	4.00	6.00
1956	Voyageur	209,092	4.50	9.00
1957	Voyageur	496,389	3.00	4.00
1958	British Columbia	3 million	3.00	5.00
1959	Voyageur	1.45 million	3.00	4.00
1960	Voyageur	1.42 million	3.00	4.00
1961	Voyageur	1.25 million	3.00	4.00
1962	Voyageur	1.9 million	3.00	4.00
1963	Voyageur	4.2 million	3.00	4.00
1964	Charlottetown	7.3 million	2.00	4.00
1965	Voyageur	10.8 million	2.00	3.00
1966	Voyageur	9.9 million	2.00	3.00
1967	Canadian Goose	6.75 million	2.00	3.00

Date	Description	Metal	Mintage	Value
1968	Voyageur	Nickel	5.6 million	1.00
1969	Voyageur	Nickel	4.8 million	1.00
1970	Manitoba	Nickel	4.1 million	1.00
1970	Manitoba, Proof-like	Nickel	646,000	1.50
1971	British Columbia	Nickel	4.25 million	1.00
1971	British Columbia, Specimen	.500 Silver	585,674	3.00
1972	Voyageur	Nickel	2.7 million	1.25
1972	Voyageur, Specimen	.500 Silver	341,598	5.00
1973	Prince Edward Island	Nickel	3.2 million	1.00
1973	Mountie, Specimen	.500 Silver	1 million	3.00
1974	Winnipeg	Nickel	2.8 million	1.25
1974	Winnipeg, Specimen	.500 Silver	728,947	3.00
1975	Voyageur	Nickel	3.25 Million	1.00
1975	Calgary, Specimen	.500 Silver	930,956	2.50
1976	Voyageur	Nickel	2.5 million	1.00
1976	Parliament Library, Specimen	.500 Silver	578,708	6.00
1977	Voyageur	Nickel	1.4 million	1.00
1977	Silver Jubilee	Nickel	744,848	3.00
1978	Voyageur	Nickel	2.9 million	1.00
1978	XI Games, Specimen	.500 Silver	709,602	3.00
1979	Voyageur	Nickel	3 million	1.00
1979	Griffon, Specimen	.500 Silver	826,695	6.50
1980	Voyageur	Nickel	3.3 million	1.00
1980	Arctic Territories, Specimen	.500 Silver	539,617	16.00
1981	Voyageur	Nickel	2.8 million	1.00
1981	Railroad	.500 Silver	699,494	12.50
1981	Railraod, Proof	.500 Silver		9.00
1982	Voyageur	Nickel	1.1 million	1.00
1982	Regina	.500 Silver	144,930	9.00
1982	Regina, Proof	.500 Silver	759,000	3.00
1982	Constitution	Nickel	9.7 million	1.25
1983	Voyageur	Nickel	2.25 million	1.00
1983	Edmonton Univ. Games	.500 Silver	159,450	9.00
1983	Edmonton Univ. Gms, Proof	.500 Silver	506,847	4.00
1984	Voyageur	Nickel	1.25 million	1.00
1984	Voyageur, Proof	Nickel	161,602	4.00
1984	Toronto Sesquicentennial	.500 Silver	133,610	10.00
1984	Toronto Sesquicentennial, Proof	.500 Silver	732,542	4.00
1984	Cartier	Nickel	7 million	1.25

Date	Description	Metal	Mintage	Value
1984	Cartier, Proof	Nickel		3.00
1985	Voyageur	Nickel	3.1 million	1.00
1985	Voyageur, Proof	Nickel	157,037	7.00
1985	National Parks-Moose	.500 Silver	163,314	9.00
1985	Moose, Proof	.500 Silver	733,354	4.50
1986	Voyageur	Nickel	3.1 million	1.00
1986	Voyageur, Proof	Nickel	175,259	7.00
1986	Vancouver	.500 Silver	125,594	9.00
1986	Vancouver, Proof	.500 Silver	732,542	4.00
1987	Voyageur	Nickel	287,330	1.00
1987	Voyageur, Proof	Nickel	179,004	7.00
1987	Loon, Aureate Nickel	Aur-Ni	205.4 million	1.00
1987	Loon, Proof	Aur-Ni	178,120	5.00
1987	John Davis	.500 Silver	118,722	11.00
1987	John Davis, Proof	.500Silver	602,374	5.00
1988	Loon	Aur-Ni	139 million	1.00
1988	Loon, Proof	Aur-Ni	175,259	6.00
1988	Ironworks	.500 Silver	106,872	10.00
1988	Ironworks, Proof	.500 Silver	255,013	12.50
1989	Loon	Aur-Ni	185 million	1.00
1989	Loon, Proof	Aur-Ni	170,928	5.00
1989	Mackenzie River	.500 Silver	99,774	6.00
1989	Mackenzie River, Proof	.500 Silver	244,062	15.00
1990	Loon	Aur-Ni	68.4 million	1.00
1990	Loon, Proof	Aur-Ni	140,649	5.00
1990	Kelsey	.500 Silver	112,026	5.00
1990	Kelsey, Proof	.500 Silver	225,867	10.00
1991	Loon	Aur-Ni		1.00
1991	Loon, Proof	Aur-Ni		5.00
1991	Steamship	.500 Silver		4.00
1991	Steamship, Proof	.500 Silver		5.00
1992	125th Anniversary	Aur-Ni		1.25
1991	Stagecoach	.925 Silver		3.00
1991	Stagecoach, Proof	.925 Silver		5.00
1992	Loon	Aur-Ni		1.00
1992	Loon, Proof	Aur-Ni		4.00
1992	Parliament	Nickel		1.00

OLYMPIC COMMEMORATIVE COINS
**The same obverse, the head of Queen Elizabeth II, appears on all of the coins.
The valuations are for coins in brilliant, new condition.**

SERIES I, 1973

Denomination	Date	Reverse Design	Value
5 Dollars	1973	Map of North America	2.75
5 Dollars	1973	Kingston Skyline	2.75
10 Dollars	1973	Map of the World	5.50
10 Dollars	1973	Montreal Skyline	5.50
4-piece Uncirculated Set, cased			16.50
4-piece Proof Set, cased			35.00

SERIES II, 1974

Denomination	Date	Reverse Design	Value
5 Dollars	1974	Athlete with Olympic Torch	2.75
5 Dollars	1974	The Laurel Wreath	2.75
10 Dollars	1974	The Greek God, Zeus	5.50
10 Dollars	1974	The Temple of Zeus	5.50
4-piece Uncirculated Set, cased			16.50
4-piece Proof Set, cased			35.00

SERIES III, 1974

Denomination	Date	Reverse Design	Value
5 Dollars	1974	Canoeing	2.75
5 Dollars	1974	Rowing	2.75
10 Dollars	1974	Cyclists	5.50
10 Dollars	1974	Lacrosse	5.50
4-piece Uncirculated Set, cased			16.50
4-piece Proof Set, cased			35.00

SERIES IV, 1975

Denomination	Date	Reverse Design	Value
5 Dollars	1975	Marathon	2.75
5 Dollars	1975	Javelin	2.75
10 Dollars	1975	Hurdles	5.50
10 Dollars	1975	Shotput	5.50
4-piece Uncirculated Set, cased			16.50
4-piece Proof Set, cased			35.00

SERIES V, 1975

Denomination	Date	Reverse Design	Value
5 Dollars	1975	Swimming	2.75
5 Dollars	1975	Diving	2.75
10 Dollars	1975	Sailing	5.50
10 Dollars	1975	Kayak	5.50
4-piece Uncirculated Set, cased			16.50
4-piece Proof Set, cased			35.00

SERIES VI, 1976

Denomination	Date	Reverse Design	Value
5 Dollars	1976	Fencing	2.75
5 Dollars	1976	Boxing	2.75
10 Dollars	1976	Soccer	5.50
10 Dollars	1976	Field hockey	5.50
4-piece Uncirculated Set, cased			16.50
4-piece Proof Set, cased			35.00

SERIES VII, 1976

Denomination	Date	Reverse Design	Value
5 Dollars	1976	Olympic Village	2.75
5 Dollars	1976	Olympic Flame	2.75
10 Dollars	1976	Olympic Stadium	5.50
10 Dollars	1976	Olympic Velodrome	5.50
4-piece Uncirculated Set, cased			16.50
4-piece Proof Set, cased			35.00

GOLD COINAGE, 1976 OLYMPICS

100 Dollars	1976	.583 Gold, 27 mm.	Unc.	75.00
100 Dollars	1976	.917 Gold, 25 mm.	Proof	155.00

CALGARY WINTER OLYMPICS, 1988

Denomination	Date	Reverse Design	Value
20 Dollars	1985	Downhill Skier	10.00
20 Dollars	1985	Speed Skater	10.00
20 Dollars	1986	Biathlon	10.00
20 Dollars	1986	Hockey	10.00
20 Dollars	1986	Cross Country Skier	11.00
20 Dollars	1986	Free Style Skier	11.00
20 Dollars	1987	Figure Skater	11.00
20 Dollars	1987	Curling	11.00
20 Dollars	1987	Ski Jump	12.00
20 Dollars	1987	Bobsled	12.00

GOLD COINAGE, CALGARY OLYMPICS

100 Dollars	1987	.583 Gold	Proof	95.00

OLYMPIC COMMEMORATIVES, 1992

15 Dollars	.925 Silver	Coaching Track	Proof	11.50
15 Dollars	.925 Silver	Speed Skating, Rings, High Jump	Proof	11.50
175 Dollars	.917 Gold	Passing the Torch	Proof	150.00

AVIATION SERIES, 1990–1994

This ten coin series commemorates famous Canadian aviators and airplanes. Each of the $20.00 coins in the series are composed of Sterling (.925) silver and .075 copper, and a 24 kt. covering of gold in the field (.8 grams). Each coin is encapsulated and in Proof quality. The obverse features Queen Elizabeth II.

Date	Description	Mintage	Value
1990	Anson & Harvard/Leckie	28,997	30.00
1990	Lancaster Avro/Fauquier	29,162	30.00
1991	de Haveilland Beaver/Garratt		30.00
1991	Silver Dart/Baldwin & McCurdy		30.00
1992	Curtiss/Jenny		30.00

1992	de Haveilland/Gypsy Moth		30.00

PLATINUM (Collector) ISSUES
All issues are comprised of .999 platinum, in Proof quality

THIRTY DOLLARS
1990	Polar Bears	1,928	65.00
1991	Owls		65.00

SEVENTY FIVE DOLLARS
1990	Polar Bears	1,928	95.00
1991	Owls		95.00

ONE HUNDRED FIFTY DOLLARS
1990	Polar Bears	1,928	175.00
1991	Owls		175.00

THREE HUNDRED DOLLARS
1990	Polar Bears	1,928	350.00
1991	Owls		350.00

GOLD COINS

Canadian Types

Head of King George V

5 DOLLARS				**10 DOLLARS**	
Date	*Amount Minted*	*Value*	*Date*	*Amount Minted*	*Value*
1912	165,680	100.00	1912	74,759	160.00
1913	98,832	100.00	1913	149,232	160.00
1914	31,122	150.00	1914	140,068	175.00

20 DOLLARS
Date	*Metal*	*Mintage*	*Value*
1967 Centennial-Proof,	.900 Gold	337,512	165.00

100 DOLLARS
All issues are in Proof quality.

Date	*Description*	*Metal*	*Mintage*	*Value*
1977	Silver Jubilee	.917 Gold	180,396	150.00
1978	Geese	.917 Gold	200,000	150.00
1979	Children's Year	.917 Gold	250,000	145.00
1980	Eskimo	.917 Gold	300,000	150.00
1981	National Anthem	.917 Gold	102,000	150.00
1982	Constitution	.917 Gold	121,708	150.00

1983	St. John's	.917 Gold	83,128	150.00
1984	Cartier	.917 Gold	67,662	150.00
1985	Big Horn Sheep	.917 Gold	61,332	175.00
1986	Peace	.917 Gold	76,409	150.00
1988	Whales	.583 Gold	52,594	200.00
1989	Sainte Marie	.583 Gold	59,657	125.00
1990	Literacy	.583 Gold	47,845	135.00
1991	S.S. Empress	.583 Gold	55,000	115.00
1992	Montreal's Founding	.583 Gold		110.00

200 DOLLARS

All issues are in Proof quality.

Date	Description	Metal	Mintage	Value
1990	Flag Jubilee	.917 Gold	18,040	200.00
1991	Ice Hockey	.917 Gold		200.00
1992	Niagara Falls	.917 Gold		200.00

ENGLISH TYPE SOVEREIGNS OR POUNDS

Normal type Gold 1 Pound pieces of English design, struck at the Ottawa Mint and with the "C" mint mark on the ground under the horse. The coins from 1908 through 1910 are with the head of Edward VII and those from 1911 through 1919 are with the head of George V.

Denomination	Year	Amount Minted	Value
1 Pound	1908-C	636	750.00
1 Pound	1909-C	16,273	125.00
1 Pound	1910-C	28,012	100.00
1 Pound	1911-C	256,946	80.00
1 Pound	1913-C	3,715	250.00
1 Pound	1914-C	14,891	125.00
1 Pound	1916-C	6,111	Rare
1 Pound	1917-C	58,845	85.00
1 Pound	1918-C	106,516	85.00
1 Pound	1919-C	135,889	85.00

MAPLE LEAF (BULLION) ISSUES
.999 SILVER, 1.000 ounce

Year	Date	Mintage	Quality	Value
5 Dollars	1988	1.12 million	Unc.	4.50
5 Dollars	1989		Unc.	4.00
5 Dollars	1989	43,965	Proof	50.00
5 Dollars	1990		Unc.	4.00
5 Dollars	1991		Unc.	4.00
5 Dollars	1992		Unc.	4.00
5 Dollars	1993		Unc.	4.00

.999 GOLD, .10 ounce

5 Dollars	1982	184,000	Unc.	36.00
5 Dollars	1983	224,000	Unc.	36.00
5 Dollars	1984	226,000	Unc.	36.00
5 Dollars	1985	476,000	Unc.	36.00
5 Dollars	1986	483,000	Unc.	36.00
5 Dollars	1987	459,000	Unc.	36.00
5 Dollars	1988	412,500	Unc.	36.00

5 Dollars	1989		Unc.	36.00
5 Dollars	1989	16,992	Proof	36.00
5 Dollars	1990		Unc.	36.00
5 Dollars	1991		Unc.	36.00
5 Dollars	1992		Unc.	36.00

.999 GOLD, .25 ounce

10 Dollars	1982	246,000	Unc.	85.00
10 Dollars	1983	130,000	Unc.	85.00
10 Dollars	1984	355,200	Unc.	85.00
10 Dollars	1985	607,000	Unc.	85.00
10 Dollars	1986	879,200	Unc.	85.00
10 Dollars	1987	376,000	Unc.	85.00
10 Dollars	1988	380,000	Unc.	85.00
10 Dollars	1989		Unc.	85.00
10 Dollars	1989	6,998	Proof	100.00
10 Dollars	1990		Unc.	85.00
10 Dollars	1991		Unc.	85.00
10 Dollars	1992		Unc.	85.00

.999 GOLD, .50 ounce

20 Dollars	1986	386,400	Unc.	170.00
20 Dollars	1987	332,800	Unc.	170.00
20 Dollars	1988	521,600	Unc.	170.00
20 Dollars	1989		Unc.	170.00
20 Dollars	1989	6,998	Proof	200.00
20 Dollars	1990		Unc.	170.00
20 Dollars	1991		Unc.	170.00
20 Dollars	1992		Unc.	170.00

.999 GOLD, 1 ounce

50 Dollars	1979	1 Million	Unc.	370.00
50 Dollars	1980	1.2 Million	Unc.	370.00
50 Dollars	1981	863,000	Unc.	370.00
50 Dollars	1982	883,000	Unc.	370.00
50 Dollars	1983	695,000	Unc.	370.00
50 Dollars	1984	1.1 Million	Unc.	370.00
50 Dollars	1985	1.7 Million	Unc.	370.00
50 Dollars	1986	1.1 Million	Unc.	370.00
50 Dollars	1987	978,000	Unc.	370.00
50 Dollars	1988	800,500	Unc.	370.00
50 Dollars	1989		Unc.	370.00
50 Dollars	1989	17,781	Proof	370.00
50 Dollars	1990		Unc.	370.00
50 Dollars	1991		Unc.	370.00
50 Dollars	1992		Unc.	370.00

.9995 PLATINUM, .10 ounce

5 Dollars	1988	74,000	Unc.	40.00 ·
5 Dollars	1989		Unc.	40.00
5 Dollars	1989		Proof	100.00
5 Dollars	1990		Unc.	40.00
5 Dollars	1991		Unc.	40.00
5 Dollars	1992		Unc.	40.00

.9995 PLATINUM, .25 ounce

10 Dollars	1988	93,600	Unc.	100.00
10 Dollars	1989		Unc.	100.00
10 Dollars	1989		Proof	125.00
10 Dollars	1990		Unc.	100.00
10 Dollars	1991		Unc.	100.00
10 Dollars	1992		Unc.	100.00

.9995 PLATINUM, .50 ounce

20 Dollars	1988	23,600	Unc.	185.00
20 Dollars	1989		Unc.	185.00
20 Dollars	1989	6,998	Proof	300.00

20 Dollars	1990		Unc.	185.00
20 Dollars	1991		Unc.	185.00
20 Dollars	1992		Unc.	185.00

.9995 PLATINUM, 1 ounce

50 Dollars	1988	37,500	Unc.	360.00
50 Dollars	1989		Unc.	360.00
50 Dollars	1989	6,998	Proof	600.00
50 Dollars	1990		Unc.	360.00
50 Dollars	1991		Unc.	360.00
50 Dollars	1992		Unc.	360.00

Newfoundland
(complete from 1865 to 1947)

LARGE CENTS
Head of Queen Victoria

Date	Amount Minted	Value	Date	Amount Minted	Value
1865	240,000	.30	1885	40,000	**4.00**
1872-H	200,000	.30	1888	50,000	**3.00**
1873	200,025	.30	1890	200,000	.30
1876-H	200,000	.30	1894	200,000	.30
1880	400,000	.30	1896	200,000	.30

Head of King Edward VII

Date	Amount Minted	Value	Date	Amount Minted	Value
1904-H	100,000	.75	1909	200,000	.30
1907	200,000	.30			

Head of King George V

Date	Amount Minted	Value	Date	Amount Minted	Value
1913	400,000	.15	1920-C	302,184	.15
1917-C	702,350	.15	1929	300,000	.15
1919-C	300,000	.15	1936	300,000	.15

SMALL CENTS

Head of King George VI

Date	Amount Minted	Value	Date	Amount Minted	Value
1938	500,000	.10	1943-C	1¼ million	.10
1940	300,000	.40	1944-C	1½ million	.10
1941-C	827,662	.10	1947-C	313,772	.10
1942	2 million	.10			

SILVER 5 CENTS

Head of Queen Victoria

Date	Amount Minted	Value	Date	Amount Minted	Value
1865	80,000	6.00	1881	40,000	3.75
1870	40,000	9.00	1882-H	60,000	3.00
1872-H	40,000	6.00	1885	16,000	20.00
1873	44,260	7.00	1888	40,000	3.75
1873-H	Part of above	200.00	1890	160,000	2.50
1876-H	20,000	12.00	1894	160,000	2.50
1880	40,000	6.50	1896	400,000	1.50

Head of King Edward VII

Date	Amount Minted	Value
1903	100,000	.50
1904-H	100,000	.50
1908	400,000	.50

Head of King George V

Date	Amount Minted	Value	Date	Amount Minted	Value
1912	300,000	.50	1919-C	100,844	.50
1917-C	300,319	.50	1929	300,000	.50

Head of King George VI

Date	Amount Minted	Value	Date	Amount Minted	Value
1936	100,000	.30	1944-C	286,504	.30
1940-C	200,000	.30	1945-C	203,828	.30
1941-C	612,641	.30	1946-C	2,041	50.00
1942-C	298,348	.50	1947-C	38,400	.50
1943-C	351,666	.30			

10 CENTS

Head of Queen Victoria

Date	Amount Minted	Value	Date	Amount Minted	Value
1865	80,000	5.00	1882-H	20,000	5.00
1870	30,000	40.00	1885	8,000	15.00
1872-H	40,000	5.00	1888	30,000	5.00
1873	23,614	5.00	1890	100,000	1.00
1876-H	10,000	7.00	1894	100,000	1.00
1880	10,000	7.00	1896	230,000	1.00

Head of King Edward VII

Date	Amount Minted	Value
1903	100,000	**.60**
1904-H	100,000	**.60**

Head of King George V

Date	Amount Minted	Value
1912	150,000	**.60**
1917-C	250,805	**.60**
1919-C	54,342	**.60**

Head of King George VI

Date	Amount Minted	Value	Date	Amount Minted	Value
1938	100,000	**.30**	1944-C	151,471	**.30**
1940	100,000	**.30**	1945-C	175,833	**.30**
1941-C	483,630	**.30**	1946-C	38,400	**.50**
1942-C	292,736	**.30**	1947-C	61,988	**1.00**
1943-C	104,706	**.30**			

20 CENTS

Head of Queen Victoria

Date	Amount Minted	Value	Date	Amount Minted	Value
1865	100,000	**3.00**	1885	40,000	**1.25**
1870	50,000	**4.00**	1888	75,000	**1.25**
1872-H	90,000	**3.00**	1890	100,000	**1.25**
1873	45,797	**3.00**	1894	100,000	**1.25**
1876-H	50,000	**3.00**	1896	125,000	**1.25**
1880	30,000	**1.50**	1899	125,000	**1.25**
1881	60,000	**1.25**	1900	125,000	**1.25**
1882-H	100,000	**1.25**			

Head of King Edward VII

Date	Amount Minted	Value
1904-H	75,000	**1.50**

Head of King George V

Date	Amount Minted	Value
1912	350,000	**1.25**

25 CENTS

Head of King George V

Date	Amount Minted	Value	Date	Amount Minted	Value
1917-C	464,779	.50	1919-C	163,939	.50

50 CENTS

Head of Queen Victoria

Date	Amount Minted	Value	Date	Amount Minted	Value
1870	50,000	3.00	1885	40,000	3.00
1872-H	48,000	3.00	1888	20,000	3.50
1873	37,675	3.00	1894	40,000	3.00
1874	80,000	2.50	1896	60,000	2.00
1876-H	28,000	4.00	1898	76,607	1.50
1880	24,000	4.00	1899	150,000	1.25
1882-H	100,000	2.00			

Head of King Edward VII

Date	Amount Minted	Value	Date	Amount Minted	Value
1904-H	140,000	1.25	1908	160,000	1.25
1907	100,000	1.25	1909	200,000	1.25

Head of King George V

Date	Amount Minted	Value	Date	Amount Minted	Value
1911	200,000	**1.25**	1918-C	294,824	**1.25**
1917-C	375,560	**1.25**	1919-C	306,267	**1.25**

GOLD COINS

2 DOLLARS

Head of Queen Victoria

Date	Amount Minted	Value	Date	Amount Minted	Value
1865	10,000	**125.00**	1881	10,000	**85.00**
1870	10,000	**125.00**	1882-H	25,000	**70.00**
1872	6,050	**150.00**	1885	10,000	**85.00**
1880	2,500	**700.00**	1888	25,000	**70.00**

New Brunswick
(All coins are with the head of Queen Victoria)

Coin	Date	Amount Minted	Value
Half Cent	1861	222,800	**15.00**
Large Cent	1861	1 million	**.25**
Large Cent	1864	1 million	**.25**

Coin	Date	Amount Minted	Value
Silver 5 Cents	1862	100,000	**7.00**
Silver 5 Cents	1864	100,000	**7.00**
10 Cents	1862	150,000	**5.00**
10 Cents	1864	100,000	**5.00**
20 Cents	1862	150,000	**4.00**
20 Cents	1864	150,000	**4.00**

Nova Scotia
(All coins are with the head of Queen Victoria)

Coin	Date	Amount Minted	Value
Half Cent	1861	460,000	.75
Half Cent	1864	400,000	.75
Large Cent	1861	800,000	.25
Large Cent	1862	100,000	3.50
Large Cent	1864	800,000	.25

Prince Edward Island
(Head of Queen Victoria)

Coin	Date	Amount Minted	Value
Large Cent	1871	1 million	.25

British Columbia
Very rare gold coins that were not placed in circulation

Coin	Date	Amount Minted	Value
10 Dollars	1862		——
20 Dollars	1862		——

(The valuations in this book are based on the coins being in G-VG condition, unless otherwise noted.)